PRAISE FOR DAVID SHIELDS'S reality hunger

"Provocative, brain-rewiring. . . . A book that feels at least five years ahead of its time and teaches you how to read it as you go."
—Alex Pappademas, *GQ*

"Maybe he's simply ahead of the rest of us, mapping out the literary future of the next generation."
—Susan H. Greenberg, *Newsweek*

"A work of virtuoso banditry that promises to become, like Lewis Hyde's *The Gift* for earlier generations, the book that artists in all media turn to for inspiration, vindication, and altercation as they struggle to reinvent themselves against the headwinds of our time."
—Rob Nixon, *The Chronicle of Higher Education*

"A rare and very peculiar thing: a wake-up call that is a pleasure to hear and respond to."
—Geoff Dyer

"This dude's book is the hip-hop album of the year."
—Peter Macia, *Fader*

"I don't think it would be too strong to say that Shields's book will be a sort of bible for the next generation of culture-makers."
—David Griffith, *Bookslut*

"One of the most provocative books I've ever read. . . . I think it's destined to become a classic."
—Charles D'Ambrosio

"Voracious and elegantly structured. . . . Entertaining, insightful, and impressively broad. . . . An invigorating shakedown of the literary status quo: recommended for readers, essential for writers."　　　　—Scott Indrisek, *Time Out New York*

"Shields has put a bullet in the brain of our ridiculously oversimplified compulsion to think of everything as a narrative."
　　　　　　　　　　—Paul Constant, *The Stranger*

"Might be the most intense, thought-accelerating book of the last ten years."　　　　　　　　　　—Chuck Klosterman

"Shields has a point. He gives a damn. He's trying to make a difference. He's using the best of his formidable talents to do that."　　　　—Wayne Alan Brenner, *The Austin Chronicle*

"Witty, insightful, and compulsively readable. Every page abounds in fresh observations."　　　　　　—Lydia Davis

"This is the book our sick-at-heart moment needs—like a sock in the jaw or an electric jolt in the solar plexus—to wake it up."　　　　　　　　　　—Wayne Koestenbaum

"Absorbing, even inspiring. . . . The ideas [Shields] raises are so important, his ideas are so compelling, that I raved about this book the whole time I was reading it and have regularly quoted it to friends in the weeks since."
　　　　　　　　　　—Jami Attenberg, *Bookforum*

David Shields

reality
hunger

David Shields is the author of nine pre-
vious books, including *The Thing About
Life Is That One Day You'll Be Dead*, a
New York Times bestseller; *Black Planet*,
a finalist for the National Book Critics
Circle Award; and *Remote*, winner of the
PEN/Revson Award. His work has been
translated into fifteen languages.

www.davidshields.com

reality
hunger

A MANIFESTO

David Shields

 Vintage Books   A Division of Random House, Inc.   New York

FIRST VINTAGE BOOKS EDITION, FEBRUARY 2011

The Library of Congress has cataloged the Knopf edition as follows:
Shields, David, 1956–
    Reality hunger : a manifesto / by David Shields.—1st ed.
       p. cm.
    1. Literature, Modern—21st century—History and criticism.
    2. Literary manifestos.   3. Modernism (Literature).
    I. Title.
    PN781.S55 2010
    809'.9112—dc22   2009030237

Vintage ISBN: 978-0-307-38797-4

Author photograph © Tom Collicott
Book design by Maggie Hinders

www.vintageanchor.com

Printed in the United States of America
10 9 8 7 6

For Michael Logan and James Nugent

I would like to express my deep gratitude for fellowships from the John Simon Guggenheim Foundation, Artist Trust, and the Simpson Center for the Humanities.

contents

All great works of literature
either dissolve a genre or invent one.
—WALTER BENJAMIN

———————

Art is theft.
—PICASSO

———————

When we are not sure, we are alive.
—GRAHAM GREENE

reality
hunger

a

overture

1

Every artistic movement from the beginning of time is an attempt to figure out a way to smuggle more of what the artist thinks is reality into the work of art. Zola: "Every proper artist is more or less a realist according to his own eyes." Braque's goal: "To get as close as I could to reality." E.g., Chekhov's diaries, E. M. Forster's *Commonplace Book,* Fitzgerald's *The Crack-Up* (much his best book), Cheever's posthumously published journals (same), Edward Hoagland's journals, Alan Bennett's *Writing Home.* So, too, every artistic movement or moment needs a credo: Horace's *Ars Poetica,* Sir Philip Sidney's *Defence of Poesie,* André Breton's "Surrealist Manifesto," Dogme 95's "Vow of Chasity." My intent is to write the *ars poetica* for a burgeoning group of interrelated but unconnected artists in a multitude of forms and media—lyric essay, prose poem, collage novel, visual art, film, television, radio, performance art, rap, stand-up comedy, graffiti—who are breaking larger and larger chunks of "reality" into their work. (*Real-*

ity, as Nabokov never got tired of reminding us, is the one word that is meaningless without quotation marks.)

2

Jeff Crouse's plug-in *Delete City.* The quasi–home movie *Open Water. Borat: Cultural Learnings of America for Make Benefit Glorious Nation of Kazakhstan.* Joe Frank's radio show *In the Dark.* The depilation scene in *The 40-Year-Old Virgin.* Lynn Shelton's unscripted film *Humpday* ("All the writing takes place in the editing room"). Nicholas Barker's "real-life feature" *Unmade Beds,* in which actors speak from a script based on interviews they conducted with Barker; the structure is that of a documentary, but a small percentage of the material is made up. Todd Haynes's *Superstar:* a biopic of Karen Carpenter that uses Barbie dolls as the principal actors. *Curb Your Enthusiasm,* which—characteristic of this genre, this ungenre, this antigenre—relies on viewer awareness of the creator's self-conscious, wobbly manipulation of the gap between person and persona. *The Eminem Show,* in which Marshall Mathers struggles to metabolize his fame and work through "family of origin" issues (life and/or art?). The Museum of (fictional) Jurassic Technology, which actually exists in Culver City. The (completely fictional) International Necronautical Society's (utterly serious) "Declaration of Inauthenticity." So, too, public-access TV, karaoke nights, VH1's *Behind the Music* series, "behind-the-scenes" interviews running parallel to the "real" action on reality television shows, rap artists taking a slice of an existing song and building an entirely new song on top of it, DVDs of feature films that inevitably include a documentary on the "making of the movie." *The Bachelor* tells us more about the state of unions than any romantic comedy could dream of telling us. The appeal of Billy Collins is that compared with the frequently hieroglyphic obscurantism of his colleagues, his poems sound like they were tossed off in a couple of hours while he drank scotch and listened to jazz late at night (they weren't; this is an illusion). *A Heartbreaking Work of Staggering Genius* was full of the same self-conscious apparatus that had bored everyone silly until it got tethered to what felt like someone's "real life" (even if the author constantly reminded us how fictionalized that life was). At once desperate for authenticity and in love with artifice, I know all the moments are "moments": staged and theatrical, shaped and thematized. I find I can listen to talk radio in a way that I can't abide the network news—the sound of human voices waking before they drown.

3

An artistic movement, albeit an organic and as-yet-unstated one, is forming. What are its key components? A deliberate unartiness: "raw" material, seemingly unprocessed, unfiltered, uncensored, and unprofessional. (What, in the last half century, has been more influential than Abraham Zapruder's 8mm film of the Kennedy assassination?) Randomness, openness to accident and serendipity, spontaneity; artistic risk, emotional urgency and intensity, reader/viewer participation; an overly literal tone, as if a reporter were viewing a strange culture; plasticity of form, pointillism; criticism as autobiography; self-reflexivity, self-ethnography, anthropological autobiography; a blurring (to the point of invisibility) of any distinction between fiction and nonfiction: the lure and blur of the real.

4

In most books, the *I,* or first person, is omitted; in this it will be retained; that, in respect to egotism, is the main difference. We commonly do not remember that it is, after all, always the first person that is speaking.

5

It must all be considered as if spoken by a character in a novel (minus the novel).

6

Method of this project: literary montage. I needn't say anything. Merely show. I shall purloin no valuables, appropriate no ingenious formulations. But the rags, the refuse—these I will not inventory but allow, in the only way possible, to come into their own: by making use of them.

b

mimesis

7

Writing began around 3200 b.c.

8

The earliest uses of writing were list-making and account-keeping.

9

In 450 b.c., Bacchylides wrote, "One author pilfers the best of another and calls it tradition."

10

In the second century b.c., Terence said, "There's nothing to say that hasn't been said before."

11

Storytelling can be traced back to Hindu sacred writings, known as the Vedas, from around 1400 b.c.

12

Homer's *Iliad* and *Odyssey,* c. 800 b.c., are epics told in verse—
not novels but nonetheless stories.

13

The aphorism is one of the earliest literary forms—the residue
of complex thoughts filtered down to a single metaphor. By
the second millennium b.c., in Sumer, aphorisms appeared
together in anthologies, collections of sayings that were copied
for noblemen, priests, and kings. These lists were then cata-
logued by theme: "Honesty," "Friendship," "Death." When
read together, these collections of sayings could be said to
make a general argument on their common themes, or at least
shed some light somewhere, or maybe simply obsess about a
topic until a little dent has been made in the huge idea they all
pondered. "Love." Via editing and collage, the form germi-
nated into longer, more complex, more sustained, and more
sophisticated essayings. The Hebrew wisdom of Ecclesiastes is
essentially a collection of aphorisms, as are Confucius's religious musings and Heraclitus's fragments. These extended
aphorisms eventually crossed the border into essay: the diaries
of Sei Shônagon, Anne Bradstreet's letters, Kafka's notebooks,
Pound's criticism.

14

The earliest manuscript of the Old Testament dates to 150 b.c.
Parts of the Bible incorporate "real things" into the text. The
laws that have come to make up Mosaic Law, for instance, were
undoubtedly real laws before they became canonical. There are
bits of song and folk poetry scattered throughout the Old Testament that seem to have had a life independent of scripture.
The Samson stories were probably folktales that the Judges
storyteller worked into his thesis.

15

It is out of the madness of God, in the Old Testament, that there emerges what we, now, would recognize as the "real"; his perceived insanity is its very precondition.

16

The New Testament renders, sometimes artistically and often from competing points of view, events that supposedly really happened. The Gospels of Matthew, Mark, Luke, and John were written 40 to 110 years after the events in question.

17

In his preface to *The History of the Peloponnesian War,* Thucydides acknowledges that he "found it impossible to remember the exact wording of speeches. Hence I have made each orator speak as, in my opinion, he would have done in the circumstances, but keeping as close as I could to the train of thought that guided his actual speech."

18

Plutarch sometimes bulleted his essays with as many as a hundred numbered sections, eschewing narrative completely and simply listing. His essay "Sayings by Spartan Women" itemizes quotations from unknown Spartan mothers, wives, daughters, and widows on a variety of topics without any transitional exposition or interpretation, or any suggestion whatsoever as to how we might read the text or even, for that matter, why.

19

In antiquity, the most common Latin term for the essay was *experior,* meaning "to try, test, experience, prove."

20

The etymology of *fiction* is from *fingere* (participle *fictum*), meaning "to shape, fashion, form, or mold." Any verbal account is a fashioning and shaping of events.

21

Ancient novels were either fantastic—Lucian's *The Golden Ass* tells of a man who turns into a donkey and back into a man— or implausible romantic adventures, such as Chariton's *Chaereas and Callirhoe*.

22

St. Augustine's *Confessions,* written in the fourth century, tells his life through the prism of his newfound faith, reflecting on his sins, begging forgiveness from God. For centuries, the memoir was, by definition, *apologia pro vita sua:* prayerful entreaty and inventory of sins. (During the Renaissance, a hybrid memoir—with a more nuanced relation to the divine— emerged: Montaigne's *Essays.* Memoir wasn't anymore necessarily what one should know but what one could know. Pascal's *Pensées.* Rousseau's *Confessions.* With the posthumous publication in 1908 of Nietzsche's *Ecce Homo: How One Becomes What One Is,* God was gone for good.)

23

The Tale of Genji: an eleventh-century Japanese text about court life.

24

In the thirteenth century, French troubadours wrote prose poems about thwarted love.

25

In seventeenth-century France, Madeleine de Scudéry (in *Arta-mène*) and Madame de La Fayette (in *La Princesse de Clèves*) wrote about the romantic intrigues of aristocrats.

26

Before the Industrial Revolution, culture was mostly local; niches were geographic. The economy was agrarian, which distributed populations as broadly as the land. Distance divided people, giving rise to regional accents, and the lack of rapid transportation limited the mixing of cultures and the propagation of ideas and trends. There was a reason the church was the main cultural unifier in Western Europe: it had the best distribution network and the most mass-produced item—the Bible.

27

When they were published, the books that now form the canon of Western literature (the *Iliad,* the Bible) were understood to be true accounts of actual events. In 1572, when Montaigne set himself the task of naming the "new" brand of writing he was doing in his journals—which later became his books—he came upon the Middle French word *essai,* meaning "trial," "attempt," "experiment." (All of life is an experiment. I love fools' experiments; I'm always making them.) Many of the most important writers in the Renaissance—Montaigne; Francis Bacon, who imported the essay into English; John Donne, whose sermons mattered much more than his poems—were writers of nonfiction. So secure was the preference for truth that Sir Philip Sidney had to fight, in *Defence of Poesie* (published after his death in 1595), for the right to "lie" in literature at all.

28

In his retirement, walking the streets of Bordeaux, Montaigne wore a pewter medallion inscribed with the words *Que sais-je?* ("What do I know?")—thereby forming and backforming a tradition: Lucretius to La Rochefoucauld to Cioran.

29

Once upon a time, history concerned itself only with what it considered important: the contrivers of significant events, on the one hand, and the forces that such happenings enlisted or expressed, on the other. Historians had difficulty deciding whether history was the result of the remarkable actions of remarkable men or the significant consequences of powerful forces, of climate, custom, and economic consequence, or of social structures, diet, geography, but whatever was the boss, the boss was big, massive, all-powerful, and hogged the center of the stage; however, as machines began to replicate objects, little people began to multiply faster than wars or famines could reduce their numbers, democracy arrived to flatter the multitude and tell them they ruled, commerce flourished, sales grew, money became the risen god, numbers replaced significant individuals, the trivial assumed the throne, and history looked about for gossip, not for laws, preferring lies about secret lives to the intentions of fate. As these changes took place, especially in the eighteenth century, the novel arrived to amuse mainly ladies of the middle and upper classes and provide them a sense of importance: their manners, their concerns, their daily rounds, their aspirations, their dreams of romance. The novel feasted on the unimportant, mimicking reality. Moll Flanders and Clarissa Harlowe replaced Medea and Antigone. Instead of actual adventures, made-up ones were fashionable; instead of perilous voyages, Crusoe carried us through his days; instead of biographies of ministers and lords, we got bundles of fake letters recounting seductions and betrayals: the extraordinary drama of lied-about ordinary life. Historians soon had at hand all the devices of exploitation. Amusing anecdote, salacious gossip would now fill their pages, too. History was human, personal, full of concrete detail, and had all the suspense of a magazine serial. The techniques of fiction infected history; the materials of history were fed the novelist's greed. Nowhere was this blended better than in autobiography. The novel sprang from the letter, the diary, the report of a journey; it felt itself alive in the form of every record of private life. Subjectivity was soon everybody's subject.

30

The origin of the novel lies in its pretense of actuality.

31

Early novelists felt the need to foreground their work with a false realistic front. Defoe tried to pass off *Journal of a Plague Year* as an actual journal. Fielding presented *Jonathan Wild* as a "real" account. As the novel evolved, it left these techniques behind.

32

The word *novel,* when it entered the languages of Europe, had the vaguest of meanings; it meant the form of writing that was formless, that had no rules, that made up its own rules as it went along.

33

In the eighteenth century, Defoe, Richardson, and Fielding overthrew the aristocratic romance by writing fiction about a thief, a bed-hopper, and a hypocrite—novels featuring verisimilitude, the unfolding of individual experience over time, causality, and character development.

34

As recently as the late eighteenth century, landscape paintings were commonly thought of as a species of journalism. Real art meant pictures of allegorical or biblical subjects. A landscape was a mere record or report. As such, it couldn't be judged for its imaginative vision, its capacity to create and embody a world of complex meanings; instead, it was measured on the rack of its "accuracy," its dumb fidelity to the geography on which it was based. Which was ridiculous, as Turner proved, and as nineteenth-century French painting went on to vindicate: realist painting focused on landscapes and "real" people rather than royalty.

35

The novel has always been a mixed form; that's why it was called *novel* in the first place. A great deal of realistic documentary, some history, some topographical writing, some barely disguised autobiography have always been part of the novel, from Defoe through Flaubert and Dickens. It was Henry James (especially in his correspondence with H. G. Wells) who tried to assert that the novel, as an "art form," must be the work of the imagination alone, and who was responsible for much of the modernist purifying of the novel's mongrel tradition. I see writers like Naipaul and Sebald making a necessary postmodernist return to the roots of the novel as an essentially Creole form, in which "nonfiction" material is ordered, shaped, and imagined as "fiction." Books like these restore the novelty of the novel, with its ambiguous straddling of verifiable and imaginary facts, and restore the sense of readerly danger that one enjoys in reading *Moll Flanders* or *Clarissa* or *Tom Jones* or *Vanity Fair*—that tightrope walk along the margin between the newspaper report and the poetic vision. Some Graham Greene novel has the disclaimer, "This is a work of fiction. No person in it bears any resemblance to any actual person living or dead, etc., etc. London does not exist."

36

When Thomas De Quincey wrote *Confessions of an English Opium-Eater,* he led his readers to believe that his addiction was behind him; he was taking opium when he wrote the book and continued to take it for the next thirty years. Edmund Gosse's *Father and Son,* written when Gosse was fifty-seven, recounts conversations that purportedly took place when he was eight; people who had known the Gosses protested that Edmund made up these conversations, which of course he had. Orwell's "Such, Such Were the Joys" was denounced for its inaccuracies by people who had been his classmates.

37

In the early nineteenth century, modern industry and the growth of the railroad system led to a wave of urbanization and the rise of Europe's great cities. These new hubs of commerce and transportation mixed people as never before, creating a powerful engine of new culture. The industrial age brought technologies of mass production. Suddenly, the cost of duplication was lower than the cost of appropriation. It was now cheaper to print thousands of exact copies of a manuscript than to alter one by hand. Copy makers could profit more than creators, which led to the establishment of copyright, bestowing upon the creator of a work a temporary monopoly over any copies, encouraging artists and authors to create more works that could be cheaply copied. Authors and publishers, including eventually publishers of music and film, relied on cheap, mass-produced copies protected from counterfeits and pirates by a strong law based on the dominance of copies and on a public educated to respect the sanctity of a copy. This model produced, in the twentieth century, the greatest flowering of human achievement the world had ever seen. Protected physical copies enabled millions of people to earn a living directly from the sale of their art to the audience.

38

In 1830, Emerson was frustrated with sermons, with their "cold, mechanical preparations for a delivery most decorous—fine things, pretty things, wise things—but no arrows, no axes, no nectar, no growling." He wanted to find what he called "a new literature." A German con artist, Johann Maelzel, visited America with a "panharmonicon," an organ without keys. He would crank its heavy silver lever three times and step off to the side, and the machine would spit out an entire orchestra's worth of sound: flutes, drums, trumpets, cymbals, trombones, a triangle, clarinets, violins. After seeing Maelzel's machine perform, Emerson called the new literature he'd been looking for "a panharmonicon. Here everything is admissible—philosophy, ethics, divinity, criticism, poetry, humor, fun, mimicry, anecdote, jokes, ventriloquism—all the breadth and versatility of the most liberal conversation, highest and lowest personal topics: all are permitted, and all may be combined into one speech."

39

In the first half of the nineteenth century, which remains for many a paradise lost of the novel, certain important certainties were in circulation: in particular the confidence in a logic of things that was just and universal. All the technical elements of narrative—the systematic use of the past tense and the third person, the unconditional adoption of chronological development, linear plots, the regular trajectory of the passions, the impulse of each episode toward a conclusion, etc.—tended to impose the image of a stable, coherent, continuous, unequivocal, entirely decipherable universe. To have a name was important, all the more so for being the weapon in a hand-to-hand struggle, the hope of a success, the exercise of a domination. It was something to have a face in a universe in which personality represented both the means and the end of all exploration. The novel of characters, though, belongs entirely to the past; it describes a period: the apogee of the individual. The world's destiny has ceased, for us, to be identified with the rise or fall of certain men, of certain families. The world itself is no longer our private property, hereditary and convertible into cash. Two hundred years later, the whole system is no more than a memory; it's to that memory, to the dead system, that some seek with all their might to keep the novel fettered.

40

"The author has not given his effort here the benefit of knowing whether it is history, autobiography, gazetteer, or fantasy," said the *New York Globe* in 1851 about *Moby-Dick*.

41

In 1859, Darwin's *Origin of Species,* which sold out the first day it was published, threatened to undermine the Bible's legitimacy, to explain the unexplainable. The Dewey decimal system was invented in 1876, although adopted slowly at first. A. E. Houseman said, "The aim of science is the discovery of truth, while the aim of literature is the production of pleasure." Knowledge was exciting, but it threatened to quash imagination and mythology. In 1910, the General Convention of the Presbyterian Church adopted the Five Fundamentals, a doctrine of five principles underlying Christian faith, a list of dogmas requiring of the faithful adherence to the inerrancy and literal truth of scripture. If we must be governed by the two-dimensional world of fact/fiction, then steps must be taken to ensure that our sacred texts land on the side of fact, that scripture not end up in the fictional cul-de-sac. We must be able to believe.

42

In the second half of the nineteenth century, several technologies emerged. Commercial printing technology dramatically improved, the new "wet plate" technique made photography popular, and Edison invented the phonograph. The first great wave of popular culture included newspapers, magazines, novels, printed sheet music, records, children's books. Not only did authors and artists benefit from this model but the audience did, too: for the first time, tens of millions of ordinary people were able to come in regular contact with a great work. In Mozart's day, few people heard one of his symphonies more than once; with the advent of cheap audio recordings, a barber in Java could listen to them all day long. By 1910, the motion picture had given actors a way to reach a much wider audience, effectively linking people across time and space, synchronizing society. For the first time, not only did your neighbors read the same news you read in the morning, and know the same music and movies, but people across the country did, too. Broadcast media—first radio, then television—homogenized culture even more. TV defined the mainstream. The power of electromagnetic waves is that they spread in all directions, essentially for free.

43

Plot itself ceased to constitute the armature of narrative. The demands of the anecdote were doubtless less constraining for Proust than for Flaubert, for Faulkner than for Proust, for Beckett than for Faulkner. To tell a story became strictly impossible. The books of Proust and Faulkner are crammed with stories, but in the former, they dissolve in order to be recomposed to the advantage of a mental architecture of time, whereas in the latter, the development of themes and their many associations overwhelms all chronology to the point of seeming to bury again in the course of the novel what the narrative has just revealed. Even in Beckett, there's no lack of events, but they're constantly in the process of contesting themselves: the same sentence may contain an observation and its immediate negation. It's now not the anecdote that's lacking—only its character of certainty, its tranquility, its innocence.

44

Collage, the art of reassembling fragments of preexisting images in such a way as to form a new image, was the most important innovation in the art of the twentieth century.

45

After Freud, after Einstein, the novel retreated from narrative, poetry retreated from rhyme, and art retreated from the representational into the abstract.

C

books
for people
who find
television
too slow

46

Abstract expressionism: the manipulation of reality through its technique of spontaneous creation on the canvas.

47

I listened to a tour guide at the National Gallery ask his group what made Rothko great. Someone said, "The colors are beautiful." Someone else mentioned how many books and articles had been written about him. A third person pointed out how much people had paid for his paintings. The tour guide said, "Rothko is great because he forced artists who came after him to change how they thought about painting." This is the single most useful definition of artistic greatness I've ever encountered.

48

In 1987, Cynthia Ozick said, "I recently did a review of William Gaddis and talked about his ambition—his coming on the scene when it was already too late to be ambitious in that huge way with a vast modernist novel." She reviewed *Carpenter's Gothic*. The "vast modernist novel" to which she was referring was *The Recognitions*. It's difficult to overemphasize how misguided her heroic (antiheroic) way of thinking is.

49

The American writer has his hands full, trying to understand and then describe and then make credible much of the American reality. It stupefies, it sickens, it infuriates, and finally it is even a kind of embarrassment to one's own meager imagination. The actuality is continually outdoing our talents, and the culture tosses up figures almost daily that are the envy of any novelist.

50

The creators of characters, in the traditional sense, no longer manage to offer us anything more than puppets in which they themselves have ceased to believe. The present period is one of administrative numbers.

51

The life span of a fact is shrinking. I don't think there's time to save it. It used to be that a fact would last as long as its people, as long as kingdoms stood or legacies lived or myths endured their skeptics. But now facts have begun to dwindle to the length of a generation, to the life spans and memories of wars and plagues and depressions. Once the earth was flat, but now we say it's round. Once we thought we could sail west to the Indies; now we know that a New World is there. Once we were the center of a vast but known universe; now we're just a speck in a vast and chaotic jumble.

52

Modernism ran its course, emptying out narrative. Novels became all voice, anchored neither in plot nor circumstance, driving the storytelling impulse underground. The sound of voice alone grew less compelling; the longing for narration rose up again, asserting the oldest claim on the reading heart: the tale. What could be more literal than The Story of My Life now being told by Everywoman and Everyman?

53

Suddenly everyone's tale is tellable, which seems to me a good thing, even if not everyone's story turns out to be fascinating or well told.

54

Plot is a way to stage and dramatize reality, but when the presentation is too obviously formulaic, as it so often is, the reality is perceived as false. Skeptical of the desperation of the modernist embrace of art as the only solution, and hyperaware of all artifices of genre and form, we nevertheless seek new means of creating the real.

55

Barbara Kruger was a painter, but her day job was photo editor at *Glamour*. One day she could no longer tolerate the divide between the two activities, and her artwork became the captioning of photos.

56

Painting isn't dead. The novel isn't dead. They just aren't as central to the culture as they once were.

57

In 1963, Marguerite Yourcenar said, "In our time, the novel devours all other forms; one is almost forced to use it as a medium of expression." No more. Increasingly, the novel goes hand in hand with a straitjacketing of the material's expressive potential. One gets so weary watching writers' sensations and thoughts get set into the concrete of fiction that perhaps it's best to avoid the form as a medium of expression.

58

My medium is prose, not the novel.

59

Just as *Stop-Time* obliges us ultimately to distinguish between Conroy the author and Frank the character, so *A Fan's Notes* requires that a similar distinction be drawn between Exley the author and Frederick the character, a distinction that much more difficult to draw because Frederick seems, throughout the course of the narrative, to be writing—or at least trying to write—the very book we're reading. Which accounts for the greater technical and structural complexity of *A Fan's Notes* and also explains why a book so carefully created and meticulously ironized was so often criticized for being autobiographically self-indulgent. It's in this very struggle between literary form and lived life that these two books find the structural tension which transforms Conroy's "autobiographical narrative" and Exley's "fictional memoir" into fully accomplished works of art. There are two unmistakable and distinctly positive effects of novels-as-autobiography like Frank Conroy's *Stop-Time* and Frederick Exley's *A Fan's Notes:* first, they deliberately undermine the traditional and largely spurious authority of the novelist by depriving him of his privileged position above and beyond the world; and second, they narrow the gap that exists between fiction and autobiography, a gap that is artificial to begin with.

60

The first essay in Bernard Cooper's *Maps to Anywhere* was selected by Annie Dillard as one of the best essays of 1988, but the book as a whole won the PEN/Hemingway Award for the best first work of fiction of 1990, while in the foreword to the book Richard Howard calls the chapters "neither fictions nor essays, neither autobiographical illuminations nor cultural inventions." The narrator—Howard calls him "the Bernard-figure (like the Marcel-figure, neither character nor symbol)"—is simultaneously "the author" and a fictional creation. From mini-section to mini-section and chapter to chapter, Bernard's self-conscious and seriocomic attempts to evoke and discuss his own homosexuality, his brother's death, his parents' divorce, and Southern California kitsch are woven together to form a beautifully meditative and extremely original bildungsroman. "Maps to anywhere" comes to mean (comes to ask): when a self can (through language, memory, research, and invention) project itself everywhere, and can empathize with anyone or anything, what exactly is a self?

61

The subtitle of Douglas Coupland's *Generation X* is "Tales for an Accelerated Culture," but the front of the book carries a blurb announcing that it's a novel. Is the book a collection of stories or a novel, nonfiction or fiction? Graphics, statistics, and mock-sociological definitions compete, as marginalia, with the principal text, which consists of "tales" only loosely connected by the same cast of characters, but very tightly organized around the inability of any of the characters to feel, really, anything. The mixture of nonfiction and fiction— information crowding out imagination—in *Generation X* embodies the idea that these characters, bombarded by mall culture and mass media, feel that they have "McLives" rather than lives.

62

On the top of each page of Brian Fawcett's *Cambodia: A Book for People Who Find Television Too Slow* appear parables—some fantastic, others quasi-journalistic, and all of which are concerned with mass media's complete usurpation of North American life (Fawcett is Canadian). On the bottom of each page, meanwhile, runs a book-length footnote about the Cambodian war. The effect of the bifurcated page is to confront the reader with Fawcett's point: wall-to-wall media represent as thorough a raid on individual memory as the Khmer Rouge.

63

How can we enjoy memoirs, believing them to be true, when nothing, as everyone knows, is so unreliable as memory? Many memoirs make a virtue of seeming unadorned, unvarnished, but the first and most unforgettable thing we learn about memory is that it's fallible. Memories, we now know, can be buried, lost, blocked, repressed, even recovered. We remember what suits us, and there's almost no limit to what we can forget. Only those who keep faithful diaries will know what they were doing at this time, on this day, a year ago. The rest of us recall only the most intense moments, and even these tend to have been mythologized by repetition into well-wrought chapters in the story of our lives. To this extent, memoirs really can claim to be modern novels, all the way down to the presence of an unreliable narrator.

64

If no formal distinction exists either way, then the defining question to be asked of memoirs concerns nothing less than the degree of truthfulness they seem to manifest. This is where today's eager appetite for self-consciousness seems contradictory.

65

The lyric essayist seems to enjoy all the liberties of the fiction writer, with none of a fiction writer's burden of unreality, the nasty fact that *none of this ever really happened*—which a fiction writer daily wakes to. One can never say of the lyric essayist's work that "it's just fiction," a vacuous but prevalent dismissal akin to criticizing someone with his own name. "Lyric essay" is a rather ingenious label, since the essayist supposedly starts out with something real, whereas the fiction writer labors under a burden to prove, or create, that reality, and can expect mistrust and doubt from a reader at the outset. In fiction, lyricism can look like evasion, special pleading, pretension. In the essay, it's apparently artistic, a lovely sideshow to The Real that, if you let it, will enhance what you think you know. The implied secret is that one of the smartest ways to write fiction today is to say that you're not, and then to do whatever you very well please. Fiction writers, take note. Some of the best fiction is now being written as nonfiction.

66

Today the most compelling creative energies seem directed at nonfiction.

67

Biography and autobiography are the lifeblood of art right now. We have claimed them the way earlier generations claimed the novel, the well-made play, the language of abstraction.

68

I'm interested in knowing the secrets that connect human beings. At the very deepest level, all our secrets are the same.

69

There are two sorts of artist, one not being in the least superior to the other. One responds to the history of his art so far; the other responds to life itself.

70

As a work gets more autobiographical, more intimate, more confessional, more embarrassing, it breaks into fragments. Our lives aren't prepackaged along narrative lines and, there-fore, by its very nature, reality-based art—underprocessed, underproduced—splinters and explodes.

71

Truth, uncompromisingly told, will always have its ragged edges.

72

The lyric essay asks what happens when an essay begins to behave less like an essay and more like a poem. What happens when an essayist starts imagining things, making things up, filling in blank spaces, or leaving the blanks blank? What hap-pens when statistics, reportage, and observation in an essay are abandoned for image, emotion, expressive transformation?

There are now questions being asked of facts that were never asked before. What, we ask, is a fact these days? What's a lie, for that matter? What constitutes an "essay," a "story," a "poem"? What, even, is "experience"? For years writers have been responding to this slippage of facts in a variety of ways—from the fragmentary forms of L=A=N=G=U=A=G=E poetry that try to mimic this loss to the narrative-driven attempts by novelists and memoirists to smooth over the gaps. The lyric essay, on the other hand, inherits from the principal strands of nonfiction the makings of its own hybrid version of the form. It takes the subjectivity of the personal essay and the objectivity of the public essay and conflates them into a literary form that relies on both art and fact, on imagination and observation, rumination and argumentation, human faith and human perception.

73

Movies now seem to be so pigeonholed. That's a comedy, that's a horror film, that's an adventure film, that's an epic, boom, boom, boom . . . down the line. I want all of it; I'm incredibly greedy. It's like preparing dinner, bringing in a lot of people—we'll have some tacos, we'll have some *cordon bleu,* and perhaps some Japanese food as well. I want to mix it all together, because I think that's what life is like, and I want to stick as much of it on the screen as possible.

74

The opposite of broadcast: the distribution economics of the internet favor infinite niches, not one-size-fits-all. The web's peer-to-peer architecture: a symmetrical traffic load, with as many senders as receivers and data transmissions spread out over geography and time. A new regime of digital technology has now disrupted all business models based on mass-produced copies, including the livelihoods of artists. The contours of the electronic economy are still emerging, but while they do, the wealth derived from the old business model is being spent to try to protect that old model. Laws based on the mass-produced copy are being taken to the extreme, while desperate measures to outlaw new technologies in the marketplace "for our protection" are introduced in misguided righteousness. This is to be expected: entire industries (newspapers, magazines, book publishers, movie studios, record labels) are threatened with demise, and most will die. The new model is based on the intangible assets of digital bits: copies are no longer cheap but free and flow freely everywhere. As computers retrieve images from the web or displays from a server, they make temporary, internal copies of those works. Every action you invoke on your computer requires a copy of something to be made. Many methods have been employed to try to stop the indiscriminate spread of copies, including copy-protection schemes, hardware-crippling devices, education programs, and statutes, but all have proved ineffectual. The remedies are rejected by consumers and ignored by pirates. Copies have been dethroned; the economic model built on them is collapsing. In a regime of superabundant free copies, copies are no longer the basis of wealth. Now relationships, links, connection, and sharing are. Value has shifted away from a copy toward the many ways to recall, annotate, personalize, edit, authenticate, display, mark, transfer, and engage a work. Art is a conversation, not a patent office. The citation of sources belongs to the realms of journalism and scholarship, not art. Reality can't be copyrighted.

75

Science is on a long-term campaign to bring all knowledge in the world into one vast, interconnected, footnoted, peer-reviewed web of facts. Independent facts, even those that make sense in their own world, are of little value to science. (The pseudo- and para-sciences are nothing less, in fact, than small pools of knowledge that are not connected to the large network of science.) In this way, every new observation or bit of data brought into the web of science enhances the value of all other data points. In science, there's a natural duty to make what is known searchable. No one argues that scientists should be paid when someone finds or duplicates their results. Instead, we've devised other ways to compensate them for their vital work. They're rewarded for the degree to which their work is cited, shared, linked, and connected in their publications, which they don't own. They're financed with extremely short patent monopolies for their ideas, short enough to inspire them to invent more, sooner. To a large degree, scientists make their living by giving away copies of their intellectual property. What is this technology telling us? Copies don't count anymore; copies of isolated books, bound between inert covers, soon won't mean much. Copies of their texts, however, will gain in meaning as they multiply by the millions and are flung around the world, indexed, and copied again. What counts are the ways in which these common copies of a creative work can be linked, manipulated, tagged, highlighted, bookmarked, translated, enlivened by other media, and sewn together in the universal library.

76

The only way for books to retain their waning authority in our culture is to wire texts into this library. The reign of the copy is no match for the bias of technology. All new works will be born digital, and they will flow into the library as you might add more words to a long story. In the clash between the conventions of the book and the protocols of the screen, the screen will prevail. On this screen, now visible to a billion people, the technology of search will transform isolated books into the universal library of all human knowledge.

77

We all need to begin figuring out how to tell a story for the cell phone. One thing I know: it's not the same as telling a story for a full-length DVD.

78

It's important for a writer to be cognizant of the marginalization of literature by more technologically sophisticated and more visceral narrative forms. You can work in these forms or use them or write about them or through them, but I don't think it's a very good idea to go on writing in a vacuum. Culture, like science, moves forward. Art evolves.

79

Facts quicken, multiply, change shape, elude us, and bombard our lives with increasingly suspicious promises. The hybrid, shape-shifting, ambiguous nature of lyric essays makes a flow-chart of our experiences of the world. No longer able to depend on canonical literature, we journey increasingly across boundaries, along borders, into fringes, and finally through our yearnings to quest, where only more questions are found; through our primal senses, where we record every wonder; through our own burning hearts, where we know better.

d

trials by google

80

I exaggerate.

81

I was on a train of lies and couldn't jump off. You wonder how I could lie so fluently to you. That's because at some level, I believed everything I was telling you. I believed I met him. I believed we met. I believed I knew his life better than any biographer, because I had imagined it.

82

Art is not truth; art is a lie that enables us to recognize truth.

83

This chapter used to be called James Frey, but along came (at pretty much the same time) JT LeRoy, then Misha Defonseca, Margaret Seltzer, Herman Rosenblat. Similar phenomena keep arriving again and again, like the next scheduled train. That million-dollar, career-exploding, trick-tease train of these so-called "misery lit" (also called "misery porn") memoirs, first praised, then shamed, each taking its turn on the double-crested roller coaster of celebrity and infamy. This just in: Oprah Winfrey duped again! It's become a national tradition, each fallout more engrossing than the book itself.

84

Identity has always been a fragile phenomenon.

85

I mean, I knew I'd never be the football star or the student council president and, you know, once people started saying I was the bad kid, I was like, "All right, they think I'm the bad kid. I'll show them how bad I can be."

86

No matter how ambiguous you try to make a story, no matter how many ends you leave hanging, it's a package made to travel. Not everything that happened is in my story—how could it be? Memory is selective; storytelling insists on itself. There is nothing in my story that did not happen. In its essence it is true, or a shade of true.

87

James Frey's freshman-year heartsickness becomes a desperado run-in with the law; getting caught with a tallboy of PBR becomes his role as head of an Ivy League cocaine cartel; his incarceration at Hazelden, brought on by his parents' concern and perhaps their own inability to discipline effectively, becomes his last chance against an addiction that is certain to consume him. The process of aggrandizement: relatively ordinary problems are overblown into larger-than-life "literature." We, too, can make a myth of our own meager circumstances.

88

The JT Leroy phenomenon turned out to be a hoax, an immensely enjoyable one at that, exposing our confusion between love and art and publicity. People were made fools of—which is useful, because a good hoax is like a good con. Though a con liberates the mark from some of his material things, it also teaches him how easily he was tricked, how ready he was to believe certain stories. To "wizen the mark" is to send him back into the world a little less wide-eyed, a little more jaded, his vision now penetrating beyond the surface of things. To enlighten us, a good hoax or con must eventually be revealed.

89

If my forgeries are hung long enough in the museum, they become real.

90

Oh how we Americans gnash our teeth in bitter anger when we discover that the riveting truth that also played like a Sunday matinee was actually just a Sunday matinee.

91

The best illness memoirs, especially those dealing with psychiatric illnesses like depression, are written, I believe, not for the purpose of a peacock display but to offer solace. I, for one, expect that my readers will be troubled; I envision my readers as depressed, guilty, or maybe mourning a medication that failed them. I write to say, "You're not the only one." I write with the full faith that the reader I envision is hungry for my talk, because I know how hungry I am for reports from the trenches, stories that might help me map my way. We must consider the illness memoir not only as, or solely as, an *Oprah* bid, but also as this: a gift from me to you, a folk cure, a hand held out. I look into my heart and see a whore there, but I also see something else. The fact is, or my fact is, disease is everywhere. How anyone could write about herself or her fictional characters as not diseased is a bit beyond me. We live in a world and are creatures of a culture that is spinning out more and more medicines that correspond to more and more illnesses. Science proves me right—the great laws of the universe, the inevitability of entropy. The illness memoir is a kindly attempt to keep company, a product of our culture's love of pathology or of our sometimes whorish selves, a story of human suffering and the attempts to make meaning within it, and finally, a reflection on this awful and absurd and somehow very funny truth, that we are all rotting, rotting, even as we write.

92

When Frey, LeRoy, Defonseca, Seltzer, Rosenblat, Wilkomirski, et al. wrote their books, of course they made things up. Who doesn't? Each one said sure, call it a novel, call it a memoir; who's going to care? I don't want to defend Frey per se—he's a terrible writer—but the very nearly pornographic obsession with his and similar cases reveals the degree of nervousness on the topic. The huge loud roar, as it returns again and again, has to do with the culture being embarrassed at how much it wants the frame of reality and, within that frame, great drama.

93

The JT LeRoy contretemps: we'll write some novels, have someone pretend to be him so that we have a huge backstory, which is what gives the whole thing a claim on anyone's heart. No one gives a damn anymore about the garret-bound artist struggling with his "truth" narrative. Contemporary narration is the account of the manufacturing of the work, not the actual work. What I'm interested in: the startling fragment, left over from the manufactured process. Not the work itself but the story of the marketed incident, the whole industry surrounding a work's buzz. We want the vertiginous details. If you think the heart is deceitful above all things, you should meet the author.

94

A frankly fictional account would rob the memoir/counterfeiter, his or her publishers, and the audience of the opportunity to attach a face to the angst.

95

What if America isn't really the sort of place where a street urchin can charm his way to the top through diligence and talent? What if instead it's the sort of place where heartwarming stories about abused children who triumphed through adversity are made up and marketed?

96

"JT LeRoy" was nothing more or less than a highly developed pen name.

97

Margaret Seltzer wanted so badly not to be the person she was (upper-middle-class girl from the Valley) that she imagined herself all the way into strangers' lives, and cared so much about bringing attention to those lives that she phrased her tale as memoir, because relatively few people care about novels anymore. Misha Defonseca, author of the Holocaust "memoir" *Surviving with Wolves*—pretty much the same thing.

98

Frey's narrative: frat boy in free fall arises from misanthropy and is salvaged by literary industry, which is now a subset of multimedia saturation, of which Oprah forms a higher denomination. Oprahcam tells us that we are all abused in some way, but we need arbiters to sift through the dirt for the story that can be marketed as emblematic. We begged Frey to produce self-flagellating myth, and he complied. Frey and millions behind him line up to humiliate themselves for the sole purpose of being marketed. It's so common to expect an abuse story that we have to stifle our yawns when we hear of further deceit, recrimination, backstabbing. Frey, that Puritan, witnessed what it means to be senseless while on drugs, but he can't admit he had fun. He made more sense when he was wasted.

99

Fragments, The Hand That Signed the Paper, The Blood Runs Like a River Through My Dreams, The Honored Society, Forbidden Love, A Million Little Pieces, Surviving with Wolves, Love and Consequences, Angel at the Fence: all in turn were used as paper tigers to once again misposition memoir as failed journalism.

100

Frey was crucified for a handful of inaccuracies in no way essential to the character and spirit of the book. All our sins are passed onto/unto him. Violence implies redemption: our sudden hatred toward Frey was due to the fact that he didn't hurt himself badly or violently enough to justify himself as self-perpetrator.

101

Kaavya Viswanathan's *How Opal Got Kissed, Got Wild, and Got a Life:* a piece of popular fiction, written quickly for undemanding young readers, displays some "similarities" to an earlier work of popular fiction for undemanding young readers. Excuse me, but isn't the entire publishing industry built on telling the exact same stories over and over again? Since when is that news? This is teen literature; it's genre fiction. These are novels based on novels based on novels, in which every convention of character and plot has been trotted out a thousand times before. When I worked at a newspaper, we were routinely dispatched to "match" a story from the *Times:* to do a new version of someone else's idea. But had we "matched" any of the *Times*'s words—even the most banal of phrases—it could have been a firing offense. The ethics of plagiarism have turned into the narcissism of minor differences: because journalism cannot own up to its heavily derivative nature, it must enforce originality on the level of the sentence. Trial by Google.

102

I don't feel any of the guilt normally attached to "plagiarism," which seems to me organically connected to creativity itself.

103

(Ambitious) memoir isn't fundamentally a chronicle of experience; rather, memoir is the story of consciousness contending with experience.

104

What I believe about memoir is that you just happen to be using the nuts and bolts of your own life to illustrate your vision. It isn't really me; it's a character based on myself that I made up in order to illustrate things I want to say. In other words, I think memoir is as far from real life as fiction is. I think you're obligated to use accurate details, but selection is as important a process as imagination.

105

Proust said that he had no imagination; what he wanted was reality, infused with something else. *In Search of Lost Time* begins and ends with the actual thoughts of the author; it's the manifestation of what the author must think, based on what he does in fact think. The book, by being about Marcel, a writer, is as much about the writing as it is about anything that "happens." I don't mean that everything we think is what we truly feel or that only in thought are we free of the lies and illusions of the world. I mean that you have a right, as a thinking person, to think what you think and that the closer you stick to the character of thought in your writing, the more license you have to claim that you're not making things up. Frey, for example, wrote but didn't think, *I was in prison for three months.* Instead, he probably thought something more like *I was in prison for three months, man; I was in fucking prison for three months; give it to them; throw it down* [their throats]; *they'll take it; they don't know what I went through; I'm tough* [goes to the mirror to make sure]," etc. That is, he made up the prison part: he fictionalized it (without first admitting to having done so).

106

Memoir is a genre in need of an informed readership. It's a misunderstanding to read a memoir as though the writer owes the reader the same record of literal accuracy that is owed in newspaper reporting. Memoirs belong to the category of literature, not journalism. What the memoirist owes the reader is the ability to persuade him or her that the narrator is trying, as honestly as possible, to get to the bottom of the experience at hand. A memoir is a tale taken from life—that is, from actual, not imagined, occurrences—related by a first-person narrator who is undeniably the writer. Beyond these bare requirements, an autobiographical work has the same responsibility that a short story or novel has: to shape a piece of experience so that it moves from a tale of private interest to one with meaning for the disinterested reader.

107

What I want to do is take the banality of nonfiction (the literalness of "facts," "truth," "reality"), turn that banality inside out, and thereby make nonfiction a staging area for the investigation of any claim of facts and truth, an extremely rich theater for investigating the most serious epistemological questions. The lyric essay is the literary form that gives the writer the best opportunity for rigorous investigation, because its theater is the world (the mind contemplating the world) and offers no consoling dream-world, no exit door.

108

In English, the term *memoir* comes directly from the French for *memory, mémoire,* a word that is derived from the Latin for the same, *memoria.* And yet more deeply rooted in the word *memoir* is a far less confident one. Embedded in Latin's *memoria* is the ancient Greek *mérmeros,* an offshoot of the Avestic Persian *mermara,* itself a derivative of the Indo-European for that which we think about but cannot grasp: *mer-mer,* "to vividly wonder," "to be anxious," "to exhaustingly ponder." In this darker light of human language, the term suggests a literary form that is much less confident than today's novelistic memoir, with its effortlessly relayed experiences.

109

Autobiography is ruled by chronology and is date-driven. It's a line running through time, punctuated by incident. The very thing that would seem to be the basis of autobiographical writing—a life over time—is not the ground the memoir can stand on. It has to root itself in the same dilemmas and adventures as poetry and fiction. It has to make a story. In doing that, it has to disregard a lot of the life. The inevitable incompleteness of memoir may account for the fact that people can write more than one memoir. Presumably, you would write only one autobiography. You can write multiple memoirs, though, coming at your life from different angles.

110

Every work of literature has both a situation and a story. The situation is the context or circumstance, sometimes the plot; the story is the emotional experience that preoccupies the writer: the insight, the wisdom, the thing one has come to say. The facts of the situation don't much matter, so long as the underlying truth resonates. Memoir is neither testament nor fable nor analytic transcription. A memoir is a work of sustained narrative prose controlled by an idea of the self under obligation to lift from the raw material of life a tale that will shape experience, transform the event, deliver wisdom. Truth in a memoir is achieved not through a recital of actual events; it's achieved when the reader comes to believe that the writer is working hard to engage with the experience at hand. What happened to the writer isn't what matters; what matters is the larger sense that the writer is able to make of what happened. For that, the power of a writing imagination is required.

111

I'm interested in the ways in which stories of suffering might be used to mask other, less marketable stories of suffering.

112

Memoir is a construct used by publishers to niche-market a genre between fact and fiction, to counteract and assimilate with reality shows.

113

Defending *A Million Little Pieces,* Oprah said, "Although some of the facts have been questioned, the underlying message of redemption in James Frey's memoir still resonates with me." However, a few days later, clearly influenced by her miffed audience, she apologized for leaving the impression "that the truth doesn't matter."

114

Stoic marketing plan: on TV, ingest a ton of shit—a form of abuse—and transcend it by finding the product that catapults you off the couch into another lie, I mean another life (celebrity).

115

Oprah has created around herself a "cult of confession" that offers only one prix-fixe menu to those who enter her world. First, the teasing crudités of the situation, sin or sorrow hinted at. The entrée is the deep confession or revelation. Next, a palate-cleansing sorbet of regret and repentance, the delicious forgiveness served by Oprah on behalf of all humanity. Fade to commercial as the sobbing witness, who has revealed harm done to or by an uncle or a neighbor, through carelessness, neglect, evil intent, or ignorance, is applauded by the audience, comforted by Oprah. Her instincts are fine, her integrity unquestioned, and she would never tell us a story that isn't true.

116

I'm disappointed not that Frey is a liar but that he isn't a better one. He should have said, *Everyone who writes about himself is a liar. I created a person meaner, funnier, more filled with life than I could ever be.* He could have talked about the parallel between a writer's persona and the public persona that Oprah presents to the world. Instead, he showed up for his whipping.

117

When Frey appeared on *Oprah* the final time, performing hara-kiri, many of the nation's newsrooms were tuned in. Even choosing what to include in a straightforward memoir involves a substantial exercise of creative license; journalists, though, don't seem too hip to this way of thinking: bad for their business, and they have a monopoly (had a monopoly) on popular discourse.

118

In the aftermath of the *Million Little Pieces* outrage, Random House reached a tentative settlement with readers who felt defrauded by Frey. To receive a refund, hoodwinked customers had to mail in a piece of the book: for hardcover owners, it was page 163; those with paperback copies were required to actually tear off the front cover and send it in. Also, readers had to sign a sworn statement confirming that they had bought the book with the belief it was a real memoir or, in other words, that they felt bad having accidentally read a novel.

119

In 2009, Oprah reversed herself again, apologizing to Frey for publicly humiliating him. Meanwhile, Frey, working with another writer, "anonymously" shopped around a young adult novel called *I Am Number Four,* which is about a group of nine alien teenagers on a planet called Lorien (Frey was born and raised in Cleveland, not far from Lorain, OH, a small city that is predominantly African-American and is Toni Morrison's hometown). Attacked by a hostile race from another planet, the nine aliens and their guardians evacuate to Earth, where three are killed. The protagonist, a Lorien boy named John Smith, hides in Paradise, OH, disguised as a human, trying to evade his predators and knowing he's next on their list. Frey is also working on *Illumination: The Last Testament of the Holy Bible,* a novel about a lapsed Orthodox Jew who suffers an accident and wakes up thinking he's the Messiah.

120

Capitalism implies and induces insecurity, which is constantly being exploited, of course, by all sorts of people selling things. Therapy lit, victim lit, faux-helpful talk shows, self-help books: all of these prey on our essential insecurity. The great book, though—Pessoa's *The Book of Disquiet,* say—takes us down into the deepest levels of human insecurity, and there we find that we all dwell. Autobiography at its very best is a serious handshake or even full embrace between the writer willing to face him/herself and the reader doing the same. At a lower level, it's a sentimental narrative about fall and forgiveness.

reality

121

These are the facts, my friend, and I must have faith in them.

122

What is a fact? What's a lie, for that matter? What, exactly, constitutes an essay or a story or a poem or even an experience? What happens when we can no longer freeze the shifting phantasmagoria which is our actual experience?

123

During the middle of a gig, Sonny Rollins sometimes used to wander outside and add the sound of his horn to the cacophony of passing cabs.

124

Have you ever heard a song that makes you feel as good as Stevie Wonder's "Fingertips—Part 2"? I haven't. It's so *real*. When you listen to the song, you can hear a guy in the band yelling, "What key? What key?" He's lost. But then he finds the key, and *boom.* Every time I hear that guy yelling, "What key?" I get excited.

125

Soul is the music people understand. Sure, it's basic and it's simple, but it's something else 'cause it's honest. There's no fuckin' bullshit. It sticks its neck out and says it straight from the heart. It grabs you by the balls.

126

The most essential gift for a good writer is a built-in, shock-proof shit detector.

127

Ichiro Suzuki, the first Japanese position player in the major leagues, has unusually good eyesight and hand-eye coordination and works extremely hard at his craft, but his main gift is that he's present in reality. If he's chasing a fly ball, he doesn't sort of watch the ball; he really, really, really watches the ball. When sportswriters ask him questions, he inevitably empties out the bromide upon which the question is based. Once, after running deep into foul territory to make an extraordinary catch to preserve a victory, he was asked, "When did you know you were going to catch the ball?" Ichiro replied, "When I caught it."

128

Don't waste your time; get to the real thing. Sure, what's "real"? Still, try to get to it.

129

Jennicam first went up in 1996; it went offline several years later. Every two minutes of every hour of every day, an image from a camera in Jenni's apartment was loaded onto the web. In her FAQ, Jenni said, "The cam has been there long enough that now I ignore it. So whatever you're seeing isn't staged or faked. While I don't claim to be the most interesting person in the world, I do think there's something compelling about real life that staging it wouldn't bring to the medium."

130

Act naturally.

131

Somewhere I had come up with the notion that one's personal life had nothing to do with fiction, whereas the truth, as everybody knows, is nearly the direct opposite. Moreover, contrary evidence was all around me, though I chose to ignore it, for in fact the fiction both published and unpublished that moved and pleased me then as now was precisely that which had been made luminous, undeniably authentic by having been found and taken up, always at a cost, from deeper, more shared levels of the life we all really live.

132

People often ask me when I'm going to make "real movies." These are my real movies. Nothing could be more real than the movies I make.

133

I've always had a hard time writing fiction. It feels like driving a car in a clown suit. You're going somewhere, but you're in costume, and you're not really fooling anybody. You're the guy in costume, and everybody's supposed to forget that and go along with you.

134

Only the truth is funny (comedy is not pretty; definition of comedy: pulling Socrates off his pedestal).

135

Nicholson Baker is a comic personal essayist disguised, sometimes, as a novelist. His work is most appealing when he lavishes more attention upon a subject than it can possibly bear: broken shoelaces, say, in *The Mezzanine* or an innocuous line of Updike's in *U and I*. It wouldn't work if, instead of a shoelace, it was the Brooklyn Bridge, or if, instead of Updike, it was Proust: Baker's excessive elaboration wouldn't be funny or interesting. His style feeds upon farcical and foppish topics (e.g., his essay on the history of the comma). Baker is an unapologetic celebrant of gadgets, appliances, contraptions, machines, feats of engineering. His pseudo-scientific lyricism serves him well—seems oddly illuminating—when he's over-analyzing the physics of straws or the opening of *Pigeon Feathers*. His point appears to be that nothing is beneath interest.

136

Attention equals life or is its only evidence.

137

Why do you take photographs so constantly, so obsessively? Why do you collect other people's photographs? Why do you scavenge in secondhand shops and buy old albums of other people's pasts?

So that I'll see what I've seen.

138

We are poor passing facts,
warned by that to give
each figure in the photograph
his living name.

139

In the end, I missed the pleasure of a fully imagined work in
which the impulse to shape experience seems as strong as the
impulse to reveal it.

140

Plot, like erected scaffolding, is torn down, and what stands in
its place is the thing itself.

141

—praise for matter in its simplest state, as fact.

142

There isn't any story. It's not the story. It's just this breathtak-
ing world—that's the point. The story's not important; what's
important is the way the world looks. That's what makes you
feel stuff. That's what puts you there.

143

Shooting must be done on location, and props and sets must
not be brought in (if a particular prop is necessary for the story,
a location must be chosen where this prop is to be found); the
sound must never be produced apart from the images or vice
versa (music must not be used unless it occurs where the scene
is being shot); the camera must be handheld; the film must be
in color, and special lighting is not acceptable; optical work
and filters are forbidden; the film must not contain superficial

action (murders, etc., must not occur); temporal and geographical alienation is forbidden (that is to say, the film takes place here and now); genre movies are not acceptable; the director must not be credited.

144

The most political thing I can do is try to render people's lives, including my own, in a way that makes other people interested, empathetic, questioning, or even antipathetic to what they're seeing—but that somehow engages them to look at life as it's really lived and react to it.

145

Verboten thematic: secular Jews, laureates of the real, tend to be better at analyzing reality than re-creating it: Lauren Slater, *Lying;* Harold Brodkey, most of the essays; Phillip Lopate's introduction to *The Art of the Personal Essay;* Vivian Gornick, pretty much everything; Leonard Michaels, nearly everything; Melanie Thernstrom, *The Dead Girl;* Wallace Shawn, *My Dinner with André;* Jonathan Safran Foer, "A Primer for the Punctuation of Heart Disease"; Salinger's later, consciousness-drenched work. And, of course, less recently, Marx, Proust, Freud, Wittgenstein, Einstein.

146

The first Resurrection of Christ is the heart of the backstory for the holiday of Easter and the original deification of Jesus. On the cross, he said that he would rise three days after his death. After he died of crucifixion, disbelieving Pilate and the Romans placed him in a cave and sealed the door with a boulder. On the third day, the boulder moved; Christ emerged and thanked his followers for their devotedness. This is where

Doubting Thomas gets his due. The risen Christ has Thomas actually feel the mortal wound (see the painting by Caravaggio). Jesus proves to all disbelievers that he really is the Son of God. He will return on Judgment Day. Up to heaven he goes, and he hasn't been heard from since. The last Christian died on the cross.

147

The writing class met every Wednesday afternoon for the past few years: twenty women, a retired dentist, and my father, in his mid-nineties (he died last year at ninety-eight). Although he was plagued by manic depression for sixty years and received electroshock therapy countless times, in almost every piece he presented himself as a balanced okaynik, Mr. Bonhomie. He always threw a stone at every dog that bit, but in one story he sagely advises his friend, "You can't throw a stone at every dog that bites." His children from his first marriage, from whom he was estranged, didn't attend his ninetieth birthday party, but now they did, bearing gifts. After forty, he was bald, but now his hair was only "nearly gone." My mother, who died at fifty-one, died at sixty. His voice in these stories was that of a successful tough guy: "She was dressed to the nines in flame-red shorts and a low-cut halter that showed her heart was in the right place." My dad, Sam Spade. His Waterloo was failing ever to see or call his childhood sweetheart, Pearl, after he had lost his virginity with a woman he met at a Catskills resort (the woman who became his first wife). In real life, at age sixty-eight, when he was visiting his sister, Fay, in Queens, Fay bumped into Pearl at the Queens Center Mall, got Pearl's number, and suggested that my dad call her. Again, he couldn't bring himself to call—which is a great, sad story. But in the story he wrote, he calls her, they get together, and

"Eleanor" tells "Herb": "Please don't be so hard on yourself. It happened. It's all water under the bridge now. You did what you thought was right for you then. I understand. Maybe I didn't then. But it's all over now. That year, Joe and I got married, so I guess it's all worked out for the best, right?" This was, according to my father, the "toughest thing I've ever written—painful. It hurt deep down just to write it, more than fifty-three years after it happened." I wanted it to hurt more. My father and mother divorced shortly before her death thirty years ago, and they had, by common consent, an extremely bad relationship. But it was now a "solid-as-Gibraltar marriage." My father, asking for time off from his boss, tells him, in a story, "I'm faced with a palace revolution, and the three revolutionaries at home are getting ready to depose the king." The king he wasn't. I wanted him to write about forever having to polish the queen's crown according to her ever-changing and exacting specifications. I wanted to ask him, *What did that feel like? What was it like inside his skin? What was it like inside that bald, ill dome?* No aerial views or easy glibness. *Please, Dad,* I wanted to say: *Only ground level, which at least holds the promise of grit.*

148

Daniel Johnston, a manic-depressive singer and songwriter whose early songs were recorded on a sixty-dollar stereo, has a cult following (recipient of praise from Kurt Cobain and Eddie Vedder), due primarily to the unglamorous, raw, low-quality production of his music, which chronicles his mental illness.

149

All the best stories are true.

150

If Tina Fey's impression of Sarah Palin hadn't been based closely on verbatim transcripts of Palin's performances, it wouldn't have been remotely as funny, and it wouldn't have affected the election; the comedy derived precisely from its scrupulous reframing of the real.

151

That person over there? He's doing one thing, thinking something else. Life is never false, and acting can be. Any person who comes in here as a customer is not phony, whereas if a guy comes in posing as a customer, there might be something phony about it, and the reason it's phony is that he's really thinking, *How am I doing? Do they like me?*

152

He is to be accepted and forgiven because his faults are the sad, lovable, honorable faults of reality itself.

153

A didactic white arrow is superimposed on the left- and right-hand panels, pointing almost sardonically at the dying man. (These arrows, Francis Bacon's favorite distancing device, are sometimes explained as merely formal ways of preventing the viewer from reading the image too literally. In reality, they do just the opposite and insist that one treat the image as hyper-exemplary, as though it came from a medical textbook.) The grief in the painting is intensified by the coolness of its layout and the detachment of its gaze. It was Bacon's insight that it is precisely such seeming detachment—the rhetoric of the documentary, the film strip, and the medical textbook—that has provided the elegiac language of the last forty years.

154

Life isn't about saying the right thing; life is about failing. It's about letting the tape play. Bio/autobio: *Boswell's Life of Johnson.* Jean Stein, *Edie. The Education of Henry Adams.* Julian Barnes, *Flaubert's Parrot.* Geoffrey Wolff, *The Duke of Deception* (compare G. Wolff's multivalent, self-contradictory contemplation of his childhood with T. Wolff's naïvely straightforward account of somewhat the same childhood: in *This Boy's Life,* dialogue is recalled verbatim from thirty years earlier—ironic, since the book is about a pathological liar).

155

After his family and psychiatrist sued for defamation, claiming that much of his depiction of them in his memoir *Running with Scissors* was invented or exaggerated, Augusten Burroughs agreed not to refer to the book as a memoir in his author's note. It would simply be a "book," identified as neither fiction nor nonfiction. Burroughs's older brother, John Elder Robison, wrote a memoir, *Look Me in the Eye,* in which their father is portrayed as a very different kind of person.

156

I want books to be equal to the complexity of experience, memory, and thought, not flattening it out with either linear narrative (traditional novel) or smooth recount (standard memoir). *In Search of Lost Time,* Mary McCarthy's *Memories of a Catholic Girlhood,* Nabokov's *Speak, Memory,* Slater's *Lying* foreground these issues by emphasizing the flawed processes of recollection of their narrators.

157

The world is everything that is the case.

158

If you was hit by a truck and you was lyin' out in that gutter dyin', and you had time to sing one song, one song people would remember before you're dirt, one song that would let God know what you felt about your time here on earth, one song that would sum you up, you tellin' me that's the song you'd sing? That same Jimmie Davis tune we hear on the radio all day? About your peace within and how it's real and how you're gonna shout it? Or would you sing something different? Something real, something you felt? Because I'm tellin' you right now: that's the kind of song people want to hear. That's the kind of song that truly saves people. It ain't got nothin' to do with believin' in God, Mr. Cash. It has to do with believin' in yourself.

159

Reality-based art is a metaphor for the fact that this is all there is, there ain't no more.

f

memory

160

In Greek mythology, Mnemosyne, the goddess of memory, is also the mother of the nine Muses.

161

Tell the story of your life that is the most emotionally cathartic; the story you "remember" is covering the "real story," anyway.

162

Reality takes shape in memory alone.

163

Memory: the past rewritten in the direction of feeling.

164

Human memory, driven by emotional self-interest, goes to extraordinary lengths to provide evidence to back up whatever understanding of the world we have our hearts set on—however removed that may be from reality.

165

According to Ulric Neisser's analysis of the structure of episodic memory, we rely—in our remembering—on complex narrative strategies that closely resemble the strategies writers use to produce realist fiction. David Pillemer, whose specialty is "vivid memories," thinks that it takes something like a painter's touch (the mind being the painter) to bring a memory to life and create belief. Antonio Damasio compares consciousness to a "movie in the brain" and argues that memories are just one among the many captions and images that our mind makes up to help us survive in the world. Remembering and fiction-making are virtually indistinguishable.

166

Anything processed by memory is fiction.

167

When memory is called to answer, it often answers back with deception. How is it that almost every warm bar stool contains a hero, a star of his own epic, who is the sum of his amazing stories?

168

Consciously or unconsciously, we manipulate our memories to include or omit certain aspects. Are our memories therefore fictions?

169

Memories have a quasi-narrative structure, constituting a story or a scene in a story, an inbuilt successiveness strong enough to keep the narrative the same on each act of remembering but not strong enough to ensure that the ordering of events is the ordering that originally took place.

170

Scooter Libby, Dick Cheney's former chief of staff, hired a memory-loss expert to make the case that Libby forgot about Valerie Plame's employment status due to the "vulnerability of memory." Libby's defense team argued that "any misstatements he made during his FBI interviews or grand jury testimony were not intentional but rather the result of confusion, mistake, or faulty memory."

171

Remembering his country, he imagined it.

172

Our personal experience, though it may convey great truths, most likely won't be verified by security camera tapes later. We usually think of memory in just this way, as if a recorder planted in our head could be rewound and replayed; however, memory often stores perceptual information in verbal forms, not images. We remember a "light blue Rambler," and yet because we have translated it in our minds into a verbal construct, we would find it difficult to retranslate the memory into an image, re-creating exactly the right shade of blue. Autobiographical memory is a recollection of events or episodes, which we remember with great detail. What's stored in that memory isn't the actual events, but how those events made sense to us and fit into our experience.

173

We tend to think of our memories as having been tucked away for safekeeping in, say, file cabinets or dusty old boxes in the backs of closets or filed away on the hard drives of computers, where they can easily be accessed by the click of a button. All it takes to remember events and objects is to open the boxes, open the files, and there our memories will be, waiting for us. Just as boxes and files molder and rot and computers become infected with viruses making the files inaccessible or corrupted, so do our memories. In a sense, all memories have been forgotten. Memories are predicated on loss. It's through the act of remembering that we bring these forgotten experiences back from oblivion. They require this rescuing because they've run their course. These experiences are complete and have been relegated to our memories. In other words, to remember is to recall what we've forgotten, but it's not as if our memories have been rubbed away by years of wind and rain like names and dates on a gravestone; instead, our memories are filled with gaps and distortions, because by its very nature memory is selective.

174

The genius of memory is that it is choosy, chancy, and temperamental.

175

To fill in the holes, we turn our memories into specific images, which our minds understand as representing a specific experience, object, or thought. Our past experiences have been dismantled, analyzed, re-collated, and then made ready for imagistic recall. The images we store in our memories are not exact replicas of what we experienced; they're what our minds turn them into. They are what we need to re-create the story, which is the full experience the image represents.

176

Freud: we have no memories from our childhood, only memories that pertain to our childhood. Is a story merely a memory of a memory? How can a memory, which is grounded in an image (e.g., a light blue Rambler) and which rings so true to me, be false? If this is false, then what is truth? And why does this matter?

177

It's difficult to separate what happened from what seemed to happen.

178

Did this happen?
Yes.
Did this happen in this way?
The answer to that, if you're a grown-up, is "Not necessarily."

179

Memory loves to go hunting in the dark.

180

Nonfiction writers imagine. Fiction writers invent. These are fundamentally different acts, performed to different ends. Unlike a fiction reader, whose only task is to imagine, a nonfiction reader is asked to behave more deeply: to imagine, and also to believe. Fiction doesn't require its readers to believe; in fact, it offers its readers the great freedom of experience without belief—something real life can't do. Fiction gives us a rhetorical question: "What if this happened?" (The best) nonfiction gives us a statement, something more complex: "This may have happened."

181

The essay consists of double translation: memory translates experience; essay translates memory.

182

For example, in Proust, who is to me at base an essayist, nothing ever happens. The only obstacles are that someone might rebuff someone else or someone might get sick or grow old, and even these are usually hypothetical obstacles. People get educations, travel, buy paintings, go on diplomatic missions, but the events are for the most part meetings between various people (or simply sightings of one person by another, sometimes thanks to a stroll or a ride in a carriage) and what these meetings bring out, on a psychological level, about life itself. How can a work be considered fiction when there's no plot? Philosophy, perhaps, or criticism, but not fiction.

183

Carpenters restore old homes to their architectural and design period, not knowing the original color of the walls. If restoring a home is like writing a nonfiction narrative, and if choosing the paint for one wall is like imagining one moment in the larger story, shouldn't we acknowledge that the house and its walls were in fact never one particular way? On a single wall, sometimes wallpaper hung, sometimes paintings stared, sometimes children penned their names, sometimes flies sat, sometimes dust settled, sometimes sunlight blazed, sometimes fingerprints shimmered. The lost story the carpenter tries to restore isn't one particular story, but a pool of possible tales, with different perspectives from different characters, told at different times for different reasons. The nonfiction writer who works to revive a lost scene adds one similar story to the collection of stories that ever existed for that moment. The entire platform of my imagination—my purpose, my hope, my intent—is different from that of a fiction writer's. I don't seek to tell the best story. I seek to tell a story that once was. I seek to fill a place that once had meaning with meaning again.

g
blur

184

I think of fiction, nonfiction, poetry, drama, and all forms of storytelling as existing on a rather wide continuum, at one end fantasy (J. R. R. Tolkien and the like) and at the other end an extremely literal-minded register of a life, such as a guy in eastern Washington—named, as fate would have it, Shields—who (until his recent death) had kept the longest or longest-running diary, endless accounts of everything he did all day. And in between at various tiny increments are greater and lesser imaginative projects. An awful lot of fiction is immensely autobiographical, and a lot of nonfiction is highly imagined. We dream ourselves awake every minute of the day. "Fiction"/"nonfiction" is an utterly useless distinction.

185

Tell all the Truth but tell it slant—

186

Genre mingling is responsible in no small measure for the moral debility of intellect and character and will.

187

These categories are plastic.
 But they aren't.
 Ah, but they are.

188

I like to write stuff that's only an inch from life, from what really happened, but all the art is of course in that inch. My books tend not to have the narrative and story you associate with fiction, but at the same time they are arranged and structured, to put it somewhat pompously, as works of art rather than accumulations of information. To that extent, I like to think they're more novel than many novels.

189

David Foster Wallace's *A Supposedly Fun Thing I'll Never Do Again* and *Consider the Lobster.* Leonard Michaels's *Shuffle.* Simon Gray's four-volume *Smoking Diaries,* which dwarf his plays. Albert Goldbarth's *Great Topics of the World.* The prologue to *Slaughterhouse-Five* is the best thing Vonnegut ever wrote. Jean Stafford's *A Mother in History.* Samuel Delany's *The Motion of Light in Water.* Rebecca West's *Black Lamb and Grey Falcon.*

190

The grist of the material is factual—a narrative with people whose names you can look up in the phone book or who have historically verifiable existences—but it's fiction in the sense that it's heavily patterned and plotted; it's structured like a novel.

191

I'm interested in the generic edge, the boundary between what are roughly called nonfiction and fiction.

192

The line between fact and fiction is fuzzier than most people find it convenient to admit. There is the commonsensical assertion that while the novelist is engaged on a work of the creative imagination, the duty of the journalist is to tell what really happened, as it happened. That distinction is easy to voice but hard to sustain in logic. For imagination and memory are Siamese twins, and you cannot cut them so cleanly apart. There's a good case for arguing that any narrative account is a form of fiction. The moment you start to arrange the world in words, you alter its nature. The words themselves begin to suggest patterns and connections that seemed at the time to be absent from the events the words describe. Then the story takes hold. It begins to determine what goes in and what's left out. It has its own logic and it carries the writer along with it. He may well set out to write one story and find that he's writing quite another. The more self-consciously language is used, the more responsive the writer is to the medium in which he works, the more elaborate that fashioning is. The naïve storyteller will burden you with a mass of irrelevancies, which get into the story just because he remembers that they happened to be there; the sophisticated storyteller will fashion his contingencies so that they support and move his story forward. That is fiction-making.

193

I have never written fiction, and this memoir may be as close as I ever get to it. No more than a biography or a novel is a memoir true to life. Because, truly, life is just one damn thing after another. The writer's business is to find the shape of unruly life and to serve her story. Not, you may note, to serve her family, or to serve the truth, but to serve the story. There really is no choice. A reporter of fact is in service to the facts, a eulogist to the family of the dead, but a writer serves the story without apology to competing claims. This is an attitude that some have characterized as ruthless: that cold detachment, that remove, that allows writers to make a commodity of the lives of others. But a writer who cannot separate herself from her characters and see them within the full spectrum of their human qualities loses everything in a haze of nostalgia. Now you may ask: *Just what is the relation of your memoir to the truth?* It is as close as it can be. The moment you put pen to paper and begin to shape a story, the essential nature of life—that one damn thing after another—is lost.

194

Good nonfiction has to be as carefully shaped as good fiction, and I'm not bothered at all by this artifice.

195

You adulterate the truth as you write. There isn't any pretense that you try to arrive at the literal truth. And the only consolation when you confess to this flaw is that you are seeking to arrive at poetic truth, which can be reached only through fabrication, imagination, stylization. What I'm striving for is authenticity; none of it is real.

196

Go, go, go, said the bird: human kind
Cannot bear very much reality.

197

We all stretch the truth and tell lies by omission. Just getting along with people involves both. Humans are hardwired to deceive. We deceive when we're competing with other members of the same sex; we deceive when we're trying to attract the other sex. Deception is more the state of nature than not deceiving. In the animal kingdom, virtually every species deceives all the time. Why don't we lie even more? It helps our reputation for people to know they can believe us.

198

There has always been something that bothered me a little bit about the invisible camera of classic *cinéma vérité*—an attempt at some pure form of objectivity that always seemed impossible and, at least in my attempts, dishonest, in some ways. In all of the hue and cry about objectivity and truth being captured by a camera at twenty-four frames per second, I've missed the idea of subjectivity. Somehow melding the two—the objective data of the world with a very subjective, very interior consciousness, as expressed through voice-over and on-camera appearances—seemed to give me the clay from two different pits to work with in sculpting something that suited me better than pure *cinéma vérité*.

199

Cinéma vérité doesn't make a clear enough distinction between fact and truth—as if facts constituted truth—but there's quite a distinction. When you read a great poem, you instantly notice that there's a deep truth in it, which passes into you and becomes part of your inner existence. In great moments of cinema, you're struck by a similar illumination. And that's what I'm after, in documentaries and feature films. You can't even call my documentaries "documentary," though; I fabricate, I invent, I write dialogue. The border line between documentaries and feature films is blurred; in fact, it doesn't exist.

200

Art is real.

I make it real by putting it into words.

201

I see every art as importantly documentary. Everything is always already invented; we merely articulate, arrange. The forms of art that make art's status as document the most explicit give me real delight. I'm inclined to say that this preference in me has something to do, also, with my lesser inclination to sign than to design. One looks not with a predisposition as to meaning, selecting items according to some prior sense of importance, but rather with an eye that roves, catching only the unforeseen patterns across a field. At least that's what the pleasure of a documentary intelligence seems to me to be. It's always, of course, a fiction: a description of the pattern-loving eye, the perceiver's ways of moving, removing, seeing, revising. Revisiting a site three times, one revisits three sites. Also, threesomes start to matter. But things matter in documentary as embodiment, not argument—at least in the documentaries I like, the least narrated ones. In documentary, more than in any other kind of film, I'm aware of the camera. Nothing short of a shot of a camera (as at the end of *Death in Venice,* the empty-headed camera apparatus on the beach) can so remind me of the missing cameraman. The missing cameraman, a presence that informs, a fierceness that's effaced—that's as close as I can get to being reminded of the strangeness of being in a body, oneself, in the world: always facing out.

202

Inherently, documentary is going to have an edge in getting at truth that fiction doesn't have, but of course if you're intelligent about it, you have to admit that there's no single truth, anyway.

203

Since to live is to make fiction, what need to disguise the world as another, alternate one? At the same time, strict reportage, with its prohibition against invention, has its own aesthetically intolerable demands.

204

As a preamble to their performances, traditional storytellers in Majorca would say, "It was and it was not so."

205

The poles of fiction and nonfiction are constantly bouncing their force fields back and forth between each other.

206

—the indivisibility of the varieties of expression.

207

The books that most interest me sit on a frontier between genres. On one level, they confront the real world directly; on another level, they mediate and shape the world, as novels do. The writer is there as a palpable presence on the page, brooding over his society, daydreaming it into being, working his own brand of linguistic magic on it. What I want is the real world, with all its hard edges, but the real world fully imagined and fully written, not merely reported.

208

Most, perhaps even all, good work (or, okay, work that excites me) eludes easy generic classification: once we know it's coloring entirely within the lines called "novel" or "memoir" or "Hollywood movie," I honestly don't see how anything emotionally or intellectually interesting can happen for the reader.

209

It's crucial, in my formulation, that neither the writer nor reader be certain what the form is, that the work be allowed to go wherever it needs to go to excavate its subject. My misreading of David Remnick's *New Yorker* profile of Bill Clinton as the first page of Miranda July's short story was more interesting to me than the story itself; the excitement of the Lonelygirl15 phenomenon resided entirely during the brief period several summers ago when you couldn't tell what it or she was.

210

Genre is a minimum-security prison.

211

Just as out-and-out fiction no longer compels my attention, neither does straight-ahead memoir.

212

I want the contingency of life, the unpredictability, the unknowability, the mysteriousness, and these are best captured when the work can bend at will to what it needs: fiction, fantasy, memoir, meditation, confession, reportage. Why do I so strenuously resist generic boundaries? Because when I'm constrained within a form, my mind shuts down, goes on a sit-down strike, saying, *This is boring, so I refuse to try very hard.* I find it very nearly impossible to read a contemporary novel that presents itself unself-consciously as a novel, since it's not clear to me how such a book could convey what it feels like to be alive right now. Instead, it must constantly be shifting shape, redefining itself, staying open for business way past closing time. "Don't mess with Mr. In-Between," my father would often advise me, but it seems to me that Mr. In-Between is precisely where we all live now.

213

In all the reconstructive or restorative arts—forensics, forensic anthropology, paleontology, archaeology, art restoration, fields into which scholars have put enormous work, defining methods, freedoms, and boundaries as they strive to fill in the blanks of history—people make the best educated guess as to what "really" happened. Archaeologists imagine the buildings that once stood upon the foundations they unearth. Forensic specialists imagine the faces that masked old skulls. An art restorer "paints over" a painting to bring it "back to the original." A police sketch of a suspected criminal is routinely derived from the imaginations of several witnesses. Similarly, imagined stories have an important place in nonfiction. Why are certain kinds of knowing favored over others in a genre in which veracity carries weight?

214

There is only one kind of memoir I can see to write and that's a slippery, playful, impish, exasperating one, shaped, if it could be, like a question mark.

215

A character is either "real" or "imaginary"? If you think that, *hypocrite lecteur,* I can only smile. You do not think of even your own past as quite real; you dress it up, you gild it or blacken it, censor it, tinker with it, fictionalize it, in a word, and put it away on a shelf—your book, your romanced autobiography. We are all in flight from reality. That is the basic definition of Homo sapiens.

216

By eluding definitive observation, he remains perpetually real and perpetually imaginary.

217

To be alive is to travel ceaselessly between the real and the imaginary, and mongrel form is about as exact an emblem as I can conceive for the unsolvable mystery at the center of identity.

218

Like a number of playwrights from Luigi Pirandello to Jack Gelber, he is attempting to bring the audience completely into the action, to make it forget what is real and what is not.

219

Mr. Winterbottom's recent films have trampled the boundary between artifice and documentary.

220

How much is true and how much is acting in this extremely intimate, fake-but-real documentary about the Wagners, a voluble, often abrasive New York couple in late middle age who drive across the country with their adult daughters to visit their son, a Los Angeles filmmaker? That filmmaker, Andrew Wagner, who accompanied them on the trip, is actually the producer, director, and cinematographer of *The Talent Given Us*. Whatever the truth, this fascinating, lively film adds a new twist to the documentary form.

221

It's always been tough getting my life and art aligned, and I firmly believe that in order to be a truly good artist, you need to link your art to your life.

222

Try to make it real—compared to what?

223

My real life has fallen into the cracks between myself and my film.

224

Richard Stern is, as one critic has said, "almost famous for being not famous"—friend of Pound, Beckett, Bellow, Mailer, Roth. Stern says, "My whole life I've pursued these people: great inventors. What is the best, the most interesting thing going? Since I was a little tyke, I've wanted to find out what makes the great tick. Growing up in New York, I trailed Sinclair Lewis up to what didn't succeed in being an escape route, I met Artur Schnabel on a bus and asked him if he'd like to use our piano, Einstein in Central Park. In England— Cambridge—the physicist Paul Dirac came over with a mis-delivered letter, so I used to cross the street and ask dumbie questions about the Big Bang. He was supposed to be laconic,

Delphic, but I found him open and fluent. Being at the University of Chicago has led to friendships with all sorts of remarkable people. Writers are usually the best to know. Their business is openness and fluency. People frequently ask, 'Isn't it bad to be in Roth's and Bellow's shadow?' I don't feel that." He doesn't feel that because his deepest subject has always been the making and remaking of actuality. By standing next to monuments and measuring them, he has produced meditations on the relation between imagination and reality that are as meaningful, powerful, profound, beautiful, and funny as any of the monuments he was measuring. A book he has cited as one of his strongest influences is Ford Madox Ford's *The Good Soldier:* the putatively pathetic Dowell contemplating the putatively heroic Ashburnham. "You make something of your limits," Stern says. "Maybe that's your signature." It's shtick: R. Stern, pro schlemiel; friend of the great, the near great, the ingrate. An interviewer asks him, "How did this brainy, intellectual, deliberately obsolete persona of yours evolve?" Stern's reply: "Boy, I'm devastated." Asked why his work isn't more popular, he says, "There's an absence of something—an energy, a breadth. A severity, a sourness. Some recusant quality which repels? A low quotient of magic? Who knows?" He quotes John Barth saying to him, "Oh, you know a lot, and you're productive, but where's the virtuosity, where's the art?" The art consists of feigning that there's mainly miscellany and little order to Stern's "orderly miscellanies," which Hugh Kenner has called "almost the invention of a new genre." In their hybrid messiness, straddling fiction and non-, life and art, Stern's "orderly miscellanies" perfectly embody and dramatize Stern's perpetual agon. The miscellanies' titles invariably define, with precision and subtlety, the thematic investigations the books undertake: *One Person and Another* is about idolatry;

What Is What Was is about memory; *The Position of the Body* is about mortality. Asked who have been the biggest influences on him, he says, "Stendhal. Proust means so much. James. Dante. Bellow: he's someone who kept going, who was disciplined. I admire that. I can already feel . . . I've had a flirtation or two with extinction. Life readies you for not living." Asked what current work he admires, Stern says, "The real stuff going on today is women's poetry—Sharon Olds writing about sex, or her feelings for her father, or her daughter, having a baby, and all that. That's big stuff." Whenever Stern starts talking about literature, he inevitably winds up talking about life; the anxious relation between life and literature is what his work always worries. Several years ago, Stern was going to visit my class, but due to a medical emergency in his family, he had to cancel and reschedule for the following year. First, though, he had suggested, "I could call you or you could call me, put me on the speakerphone, perhaps with microphone amplifier. I would apologize to the audience, speaking about the way life erupts and how dealing with it is one thing literature does, and then I would like—if possible—to read my story 'Wissler Remembers' over the phone and . . ." On and on his email went, deliriously trapped in the interstices between life and art.

225

It's all in the art. You get no credit for living.

226

The life we live is not enough of a subject for the serious artist; it must be a life with a leaning, a life with a tendency to shape itself only in certain forms.

227

In *The Shadow*, also known as *The Detective*, the French photographer and conceptual artist Sophie Calle arranges for her mother to hire a detective, who follows Calle and documents her movements; the detective doesn't know that Calle is aware of him. In *Venetian Suite*, Calle meets a man at a party and decides to follow him to Venice, where she stalks him throughout the city, taking photographs and chronicling his movements. At the end of the experiment, she confronts the man. *The Hotel:* she takes a job as a chambermaid. Before she cleans each room, she photographs and documents what each visitor has brought and in what state he or she has left the room, drawing conclusions about each person. *Dominique V* is Calle's investigation into the disappearance of a woman who told Calle she wanted to be just like her. There has been a fire in the woman's apartment, and she has disappeared. Calle photographs the scene and compares it to the charred portraits and photos the woman took before she had vanished. In *Journey to California,* a man writes Calle a fan letter, saying he's heartbroken and wants nothing more than to sleep in Calle's bed. She ships her bed to him in California. The two keep in contact over the next six months. The bed is returned. The work documents the journey the bed took. *The Sleepers:* Calle invites twenty-eight random strangers to take turns sleeping in her bed. She interviews and photographs them, displaying the results in an exhibit. *Double Game:* Paul Auster, who based a fictional character on Calle, assists the artist in her attempt to imitate the life of Auster's fictional character. Calle documents each step of the crossing and recrossing of the border between fiction and reality. *The Stripper:* Calle takes a job as a stripper. A friend photographs her, the crowd, and the milieu. In *The Blind,* Calle asks several blind people to define what they think beauty is. She posts each of their responses next to a photo of each subject. *The Address Book* (much my favorite): Calle finds an address book. Before returning it to the owner, she photographs its pages, then calls everyone in the book. She asks each of them to describe the owner of the book, his habits, qualities, idiosyncrasies, creating a portrait of the man via these interviews. The man is upset when he discovers what she has done. *No Sex Last Night* is her video of a trip she takes across the United States with a man. The relationship between the two is nearly over. They marry in Las Vegas, but the marriage lasts only until the end of the journey. In *Take Care of Yourself,* one hundred seven women interpret a breakup email Calle received on the last day of a love affair. In *Last Seen* and *Ghosts,* Calle asks people to describe pictures that had been removed or stolen from a museum, then she places the museumgoers' responses in the empty spaces. *Public Places, Private Spaces:* she travels to Jerusalem, where she asks both Israelis and Palestinians to share a public place with her that they consider sacred. Her audience isn't sure if the transformation is supposed to occur within the artwork or themselves. Calle: "These projects are a way for me to have emotions which I can control because I can decide in a way when it's going to stop, whereas in normal life I can't control my emotions as easily. I was always curious. I could watch people sleep even when their wives didn't, because it was art. Now it's a way of life. I no longer ask myself what I'm doing, but I'm not obsessed with whether it really is art. For me, it's a game; it's the critics' decision to call it art."

228

Usually I'm pretty honest. I say I'm doing a series of portraits of young women, and I want to do one of her. I explain that it's about her, but it's also about myself, and the tension this creates. I look at her, seeing myself in her and also being really into the character that she is in real life—a character that's based in truth, but a character that is also prompted by the fantasy the photographs project on her. I would rarely use an actress to play the role of a drifter. Nor would I go and find an actual homeless girl, but there are elements of these characters in the person I find that I'm really responding to and that I want to preserve through the photographs. I've never been completely straightforward; I like work that frustrates me. I don't like things that are spelled out, and whenever I feel like I'm spelling things out too easily, I'll back away and try to make it confusing for myself.

229

Because they live in a nation in which it's virtually impossible for a novel to be both interesting and popular enough to create a scandal, American novelists are drawn to the work of succès de scandale photographers. Ann Beattie wrote the introduction to Sally Mann's *At Twelve,* then produced a novel, *Picturing Will,* that contains unmistakable parallels to Mann's life and work. Reynolds Price wrote the afterword to Mann's *Immediate Family,* her book of photographs of her three children in various stages of undress and prepubescent sensuality. Jayne Anne Phillips's essay "A Harvest of Light" prefaces Jock Sturges's *The Last Day of Summer,* photographs that the FBI confiscated as "child pornography." The epigraph to Kathryn Harrison's novel *Exposure* is a Diane Arbus aphorism—"A photograph is a secret about a secret; the more it tells you, the less you know"—and the book concerns Ann Rogers, the thirty-three-year-old daughter of Edgar Rogers, a retrospective of whose photographs has been scheduled at the Museum of Modern Art. The photographs document Ann, as a child, in poses of "self-mutilation and sexual play."

230

Photography: the prestige of art and the magic of the real.

231

Part of the American character is the urge to push at boundaries.

232

I can see why you're a Miss Nude USA regional finalist. You have beautiful, long, silky blue-black hair, a perfect pout, and a gorgeous body. Please send me the color photos you mentioned of yourself in fur, leather, lingerie, garter belt, and heels. Thank you. Payment enclosed.

233

Biopic: spit-shined, streamlined narrative; caricature as character; hyper-fake as a way to get at essence of real—exactly reminiscent in all these ways of porn.

234

The lives in memoirs often have clean lines, like touched-up photographs. They glow in the dark. Does the pursuit of dramatic effects enhance the truth or bend it?

235

The Fun Effects feature included with Kodak's EasyShare software can make people in photos appear at once lifelike and, somehow, larger than life—which is all we want from art: reality, mysteriously deepened.

236

What does it mean to set another person before the camera, trying to extract something of his or her soul? When are we exploiting? When are we caressing? Are they the same? Maybe it's impossible not to do both. Maybe that's the truth of human relationships.

237

Do you promise to tell the truth, the whole truth, and nothing but the truth?

I could go on about this forever.

h

now

238

The contemporary vogue of not tucking in your shirttail (which I dutifully follow): a purposeful confusion of the realms.

239

Living as we perforce do in a manufactured and artificial world, we yearn for the "real," semblances of the real. We want to pose something nonfictional against all the fabrication—autobiographical frissons or framed or filmed or caught moments that, in their seeming unrehearsedness, possess at least the possibility of breaking through the clutter. More invention, more fabrication aren't going to do this. I doubt very much that I'm the only person who's finding it more and more difficult to want to read or write novels.

240

The mimetic function in art hasn't so much declined as mutated. The tools of metaphor have expanded. As the culture becomes more saturated by different media, artists can use larger and larger chunks of the culture to communicate. Warhol's Marilyn Monroe silk screens and his *Double Elvis* work as metaphors because their images are so common in the culture that they can be used as shorthand, as other generations would have used, say, the sea. Marilyn and Elvis are just as much a part of the natural world as the ocean and a Greek god are. Anything that exists in the culture is fair game to assimilate into a new work, and having preexisting media of some kind in the new piece is thrilling in a way that "fiction" can't be.

241

The body gets used to a drug and needs a stronger dose in order to experience the thrill. An illusion of reality—the idea that something really happened—is providing us with that thrill right now. We're riveted by the (seeming) rawness of something that appears to be direct from the source, or at least less worked over than a polished mass-media production.

242

Our culture is obsessed with real events because we experience hardly any.

243

We're overwhelmed right now by calamitous information. The real overwhelms the fictional, is incomparably more compelling than an invented drama.

244

I'm finding it harder to just "write." The seeking and sculpting of found text or sound have become my primary "artistic" function. Actually generating that text or music seems increasingly difficult. Lately I'll sit down with a blank pad and feel like I really have to dig down deep to get my own voice to come out over the "sample choir." It's a very strange feeling, like a conductor trying to sing over the orchestra, and is, I believe, a fairly new one for artists.

245

The culture disseminates greater and greater access to the technology that creates various forms of media. The "ordinary" person's cult of personal celebrity is nurtured by these new modes of communication and presentation and representation. We're all secretly practicing for when we, too, will join the ranks of the celebrated. There used to be a monopoly on the resources of exposure. The rising sophistication of the nonexpert in combination with the sensory overload of the culture makes reality-based and self-reflexive art appealing now. There are little cracks in the wall, and all of us "ordinary" people are pushing through like water or, perhaps, weeds.

246

Kathy Griffin, for example, now acts out her own reality show, *My Life on the D-List,* free from the constraints of a network time slot or a staged setting like a boardroom or desert island.

247

We are now, officially, lost.

i

the
reality-based
community

248

We're living in a newsy time.

249

We live in difficult times; art should be difficult (my goal is to make every paragraph as discomfiting as possible).

250

Tying my shoes in the lobby of the recreation center, I saw someone reading what looked like *Checkpoint*, Nicholson Baker's novel about a man who fantasizes about assassinating then president George W. Bush. I'd just finished reading the book, so I said, "Are you reading *Checkpoint*? How do you like it?" The reader seemed wary and was strikingly reluctant to respond with any specificity to my question. He asked if I was the writer David Shields. I am, the one, the only (actually, there's at least one other writer named David Shields, a scholar who's the author of a book called *Oracles of Empire*). Still, we talked about *Checkpoint* and Baker only circumlocutiously. When I was ready to go, I well-meaningly but ill-advisedly said, "I'm David Shields; I guess you know that. What's your name?"— which, of course, reanimated the entire spy-vs.-spy subtext, so he said, very slowly, "I'm Wes." No last name. End of conversation. A new moment in the republic, so far as I could tell.

251
Shortly after 9/11, the Defense Department hired Renny Harlin, the writer-director of *Die Hard 2,* to game-plan potential doomsday scenarios; in other words, fiction got called to the official aid, reinforcement, and rescue of real life, as if real life weren't always fiction in the first place.

252
I have invited my fellow documentary nominees on the stage with us, and they're here in solidarity with me because we like nonfiction. We like nonfiction because we live in fictitious times.

253
People like you are in what we call the reality-based community. You believe that solutions emerge from judicious study of discernible reality. That's not the way the world really works anymore. We're an empire now, and when we act, we create our own reality. And while you're studying that reality (judiciously, as you will), we'll act again, creating other realities, which you can study, too, and that's how things will sort out. We're history's actors, and you—all of you—will be left to just study what we do.

254

The person who loses the presidential election is the person who seems most fictional. In 2000, Gore simply was Mr. Knightley from *Emma*. So, too, in 2004, Kerry—Lord Bertram from *Mansfield Park*. During the 2008 presidential election, reality hunger in the face of nonstop propaganda resulted in regime change. Obama won because of his seeming commitment to reality, the common sense of his positions. Obama came off as completely real, playing basketball and texting people on his BlackBerry and tearing up over his grandmother's death. Both Hillary and McCain campaigned with all the logic of a Successories poster: they appeared to believe they could will their presidency into being simply by desiring it; no matter how behind they were by every real-world metric, they could still win by wishing it so.

255

Facts now seem important.

256

Facts have gravitas.

257

The illusion of facts will suffice.

258

In our hunger for all things true, we make the facts irrelevant.

j

hip-hop

259

Genius borrows nobly.

260

Good poets borrow; great poets steal.

261

Art is theft.

262

Why is hip-hop stagnant right now, why is rock dead, why is the conventional novel moribund? Because they're ignoring the culture around them, where new, more exciting forms of narration and presentation and representation are being found (or rediscovered).

263

American R & B was enormously popular in Jamaica in the 1950s, but none of the local musicians could play it authentically. The music culture was based around DJs playing records at public dances; huge public-address systems were set up for these dances. DJs started acting more and more as taste editors, gaining reputations for the distinct type of record each of them would play. After a while, the act of playing the records also became an opportunity for style and artistic expression. They still used only one record player, but they developed special techniques of switching records in a split second to keep the music going seamlessly. The Jamaican music industry started producing its own recordings, and they, too, were utilized by these sound-system men, who would make recordings specifically for their own dances and wouldn't let anyone else have the record. Even when Jamaican musicians were available to play these public dances, the audience preferred the manipulation and combination of prerecorded material.

264

Sampling, the technique of taking a section of existing, recorded sound and placing it within an "original" composition, is a new way of doing something that's been done for a long time: creating with found objects. The rotation gets thick. The constraints get thin. The mix breaks free of the old associations. New contexts form from old. The script gets flipped.

265

In the 1960s, dub reggae—artists recording new parts over preexisting music, often adding new vocals and heavy tape echo—evolved straight out of the sound-system DJ movement, which was always eager to incorporate any new advancement in technology. A decade later, King Tubby and Lee "Scratch" Perry began deconstructing recorded music. Using extremely primitive, predigital hardware, they created what they called versions. In 1962, Jamaica was granted its full independence from Britain, and more Jamaicans started coming to the United States. It was only natural that these immigrants would gravitate toward the ready-made black communities in America, especially New York City. Newly arriving Jamaicans brought with them the idea of the sound-system DJ; filtered through an African American perspective, the music moved in a different direction than it had in Jamaica. In many ways, hip-hop was born out of the Jamaican idea of turning record-playing into an art form.

266

From when I first met King Tubby and see him work, I knew there was a man with a great deal of potential. He could make music outta the mistakes people bring him, like every spoil is a style to King Tubby. He would drop out the bits where a man sing a wrong note and bring up another instrument or drop out everything for pure bass and drum riddim; then he'd bring back in the singing. You would never know there was a mistake there because he drop in and out of tracks like that's what he was always intending to do. He do it all live, too. He don't build it up bit by bit, him jus' leggo the tape and do his thing. You watch him, it like watching a conductor or a maestro at work. And of course every time it would be different. He always want to surprise people—I think he even want to surprise himself sometimes—and if he mix the same tune a dozen times, you will have twelve different version.

267

In the early 1970s, many technologies became much more widely available to the general public, including the portable

PA system, the multichannel mixer, and the magnet-drive turntable made by the Technics company.

268

You don't need a band to do this stuff. You steal somebody else's beats, then—with just turntables and your own mouth— you mix and scratch the shit up to the level your own head is at.

269

Lil Wayne, Nine Inch Nails, Radiohead are hugely popular artists who recently circumvented the music business establishment by giving their music directly to their audience for free on the web. The middle man has been cut out; listeners get a behind-the-scenes peek at work in progress. Lil Wayne can put out whatever he pleases, whenever he pleases, and the music fan gets access to far more material than a standard album release would provide. For all three of these acts, sales went up after they had first given away some, if not all, of the new release. Their fans rewarded them for creating this intimate link.

270

In 2008, Damien Hirst, the richest visual artist in the world, sold his work "directly" to buyers through a Sotheby's auction rather than through the time-honored method of galleries; it was the largest such sale ever: 287 lots, $200 million.

271

What's appropriation art?

It's when you steal but make a point of stealing, because by changing the context you change the connotation.

272

Reality-based art hijacks its material and doesn't apologize.

273

My taste for quotation, which I have always kept—why reproach me for it? People, in life, quote what pleases them. Therefore, in our work, we have the right to quote what pleases us.

274

Elaine Sturtevant, an American artist born in 1930 in Lakewood, OH, has achieved recognition for works that consist entirely of copies of other artists' works—Beuys, Warhol, Stella, Gonzalez-Torres, etc. In each case, her decision to start copying an artist happened well before the artist achieved wide recognition. Nearly all of the artists she has chosen to copy are now considered major artists.

275

Looking for songs to sample and melodies to use—picking through the cultural scrap heap for something that appealed to me—I went through the *Billboard* R & B charts and the Top 40 charts from the late 1940s until the present. With the aid of the search function on iTunes, I was able to hear a twenty-second section of just about any song I wanted to hear. It was fascinating to watch popular music morph and mutate year by year, especially on the R & B charts (black music has always been quicker to incorporate new songs and technologies). It was like watching stop-animation film footage, seeing this object (the main style of the time) grow and shrink like a plant, rise and fall, swell and collapse: swing music slimming down and splicing into gospel and making rhythm and blues, rhythm and blues slowing down into soul, soul hardening into funk, funk growing into disco, and disco collapsing under its own sheen as hip-hop hid in the underground. It wasn't until after I'd gone through the whole set of charts and reviewed my notes that I realized there was a trend in the songs I chose to sample. The number of songs I picked remained consistent through the 1950s and '60s, but by the end of the '70s it dropped off. I'd picked only a few songs from the '80s and none from the '90s. Why do the songs of the late '70s and afterward hold very little appeal for me? Somewhere along the way, as recording technology got better and better each year, the music lost something; it became too perfect, too complete. Which is why so many artists have turned to using samples and other preexisting sources in various forms: in this rush of technological innovation, we've lost something along the way and are going back to try to find it, but we don't know what that thing is. Eating genetically altered, neon-orange bananas, we aren't getting what we need, and we know something is missing. We're clinging to anything that seems "real" or organic or authentic. We want rougher sounds, rougher images, raw footage, uncensored by high technology and the powers that be.

276

Rappers got the name MC (master of ceremonies) because they began as hosts at public dances, and as the form evolved, they began to take more and more liberties in what they said between and over the records. Emceeing evolved into a channel for artistic expression—the voice of the host or the voice of the editor fusing with the selected program. The materials of art now include bigger clumps of cultural sediment. Everything in the history of media is fair game: artists painting pictures over road maps, placing photos within comic book landscapes, Kanye West splicing together his own song "Gold Digger" with Ray Charles's "I Got a Woman." It's exciting to deface things that we live among, whether what's defaced is an Otis Redding record or a brick wall.

277

The birth of jazz: musicians made new use of what was available—marching-band instruments left over from the Spanish-American War. Jazz also made use of different forms of music, from ragtime to blues and impressionistic classical music. Later, jazz ran improvisatory riffs on show-tune standards. Or think of a cover version: a composition that already exists is revisioned by another artist. The original composition still exists, and the new one dances on top of the old one, like an editor writing notes in the margins. Hip-hop and dance DJs take snatches of different songs that already exist in the culture and stitch them together to suit their own needs and moods. The folk tradition in action: finding new uses for things by selecting the parts that move you and discarding the rest.

278

Facebook and MySpace are crude personal essay machines. On everyone's Facebook page is a questionnaire, on which each person is asked to list personal info—everything from age to sexual status. A MySpace user can choose a sound track for his page, post pictures of himself, post downloads, and redesign the graphics however he wishes. Many people update their pages constantly and provide running commentary on their lives in the blog function that comes with a site. Millions of little advertisements for the self. I learn more about my younger brothers from reading their Facebook pages than I ever have from actual conversation with them. They write detailed accounts of their personalities and take everything very seriously (as many do) in a sincere attempt to communicate with others but also to control the presentation of their "image." Every page is a bent version of reality—too unsophisticated to be art but too self-conscious to be mere reportage. In this new landscape, everyone gets a channel. It seems to be the ultimate destiny of every medium to be dragged down to the lowest common denominator, which is at once democratic, liberating, exhilarating, bland, deafening, and confusing. User-made content is the new folk art. If an eighteen-year-old girl in Delaware can't be in a Hollywood movie, she takes pictures of herself dressed how she imagines a movie star would dress and posts them on her MySpace page. If the members of a Missoula bar band can never be on MTV, they borrow their boss's camcorder, make their own video, and post it on YouTube. Reality-based art by necessity. Me Media. Blogs, wikis, social-networking sites, podcasts, vlogs, message boards, email groups, iMovie, Twitter, Flickr: more than a third of adult American internet users have created original content and posted it on the web. And it gets more sophisticated every day: chain email gives way to the blog, which gives way to the vlog, which gives way to the webisode. The massively popular video games *Guitar Hero* and *Rock Band* not only turn once static content into an interactive experience, but the newer versions have extra functions to let the players actually create new music with the building blocks the game provides. YouPorn, a free YouTube-like site on which users post their homemade porn, has become one of the most popular porn sites. Karaoke is another example of how reality-based art is winning at a grass-roots level, among nonexperts. Karaoke is a generic version of live hip-hop. Little skill or equipment is needed to allow people to perform, but no matter how bad or ill-advised the karaoke singer is, he or she is using existing material for means of self-expression, and the audience accepts the fact that there is no band and the music is recorded. The song already exists in the culture and is known to all involved. What is also known is that the music itself has been rerecorded and is a bastardized version of the original backing track. Everyone knows there is nothing original going on, but somehow the whole thing becomes original in its dizzying amateurness. What happens in karaoke is a disposable variation on something iconic in the culture, such as a big '80s hit like "Billie Jean." It's reality-based art nearly devoid of art. The only self-expression is the uniqueness of the particular rendition that the karaoke singer performs. And within the space of the original hit, anything goes: squealing, shouting, changing lyrics, wishing friends happy birthday—whatever the singer chooses to do with his three minutes of spotlight. For some it's just a gag, but others take it very seriously. There's a communal feeling between audience and singer, because they're interchangeable.

279

From age thirteen to twenty-four I was in a four-piece rock band (same model as the Beatles through Nirvana). I came to Seattle at eighteen, playing that form of music, but at some point I felt there was nothing else—nothing more—to be done with the standard rock format. The band broke up, and I had a year to float around artistically. The fusion of hip-hop techniques and rock 'n' roll seemed to be much more exciting. When I came out with the new sound, many of my old friends in rock bands thought I was selling out. It was a tough jump to make. Many musicians said if I was using loops of other recordings, I was unoriginal or untalented or hiding behind technology. There was definitely a line in the sand, and when I crossed it, there was no returning to traditional rock.

280

Language is a city, to the building of which every human being has brought a stone, yet each of us is no more to be credited with the grand result than the acaleph which adds a cell to the coral reef that is the basis of the continent.

281

Just as the letters of our language are metaphors for specific sounds, and words are metaphors for specific ideas, shards of the culture itself now form a kind of language that most everyone knows how to speak. Artists don't have to spell things out; it's much faster to go straight to the existing material—film footage, library research, wet newspapers, vinyl records, etc. It's the artist's job to mix (edit) the fragments together and, if needed, generate original fragments to fill in the gaps. For example, when Danger Mouse's *The Grey Album* was released in 2004, listeners heard the Beatles chopped up and re-presented underneath the contemporary rapper Jay-Z's vocals. The album simultaneously reflected back to the Beatles, to Jay-Z's 2003 *The Black Album* (from which the vocals were taken), and to the artistic tastes of the professional DJ who made the new piece of art. The songs work as songs, but they also work as history lessons. Another layer was added by the fact that it's illegal to use the Beatles for sampling. Capitol Records went to court to silence the album, but it was already too far out into the culture to be stopped. Beyond the use of old media to make a new project, there was the added benefit of a "plotline" on top of the music (underground art vs. corporate empire). This combination led to record-setting free downloads.

282

The DJ known as Girl Talk is taking sampling to its inevitable extreme. He runs Lil Wayne over Nirvana, Elton John over The Notorious B.I.G. Sometimes the juxtaposition is fantastic; usually it's not. The novelty wears thin very quickly. Anyone can throw together two random things and call it collage art. When musical artists began using existing recordings as a medium of creative expression, they created a new subclass of musicians. An artist making use of samples, while going by a variety of names, is, essentially, a creative editor, presenting selections by other artists in a new context and adding notes of his own.

283

A literary equivalent would be along the lines of "creative translation" such as Ezra Pound's *Homage to Sextus Propertius,* in which Pound picked through the elegies of Propertius, translated them, cut them up, and reassembled them in a fashion he deemed entertaining and relevant. Examples from other forms: *Thelonius Monk Plays Duke Ellington,* in which Monk takes great liberties with Ellington's songbook. Lichtenstein's appropriation of comic book art. Picasso's use of newsprint, among other media, in, say, *Composition with Fruit, Guitar, and Glass. Paul's Boutique:* The Beastie Boys, Dust Brothers, and Mario Caldato, Jr., sample from more than 100 sources, including Led Zeppelin, the Beatles, James Brown, and Sly & the Family Stone. Steve Reich's "Different Trains," which incorporates audio recordings about train travel by Holocaust survivors and a Pullman porter. Musique concrète—for instance, John Cage's "Imaginary Landscape No. 4," written for 12 radios, each played by 2 people (one to tune the channel and one to control volume and timbre). A conductor controls the tempo; the audience hears whatever is on the radio in that city on that day. Russian composer Sofia Gubaidulina's "Offertium," which mutates themes from Bach's "Musical Offering" until they're beyond recognition. In "Three Variations on the Canon in D Major by Johann Pachelbel," Brian Eno bends and twists Pachelbel. The nineteenth-century Christian hymn "Nearer, My God, to Thee" was "put together" by Eliza Flower, whose sister, Sarah Flower Adams, had written the lyrics in the form of a poem. Eliza set Sarah's poem to the music of Lowell Mason's "Bethany." Over the years, it's been set to other tunes as well. Eliza Flower never gets credit for writing the song, credit going only to Adams for the lyrics and Mason for the music, although it was Flower who "edited" the two together.

284

In hip-hop, the mimetic function has been eclipsed to a large extent by manipulation of the original (the "real thing"): theft without apology—conscious, self-conscious, conspicuous appropriation.

285

Graffiti artists use the stuff of everyday life as their canvas—walls, dumpsters, buses. A stylized representation is placed on an everyday object. In visual art, as in other media, artists take unfiltered pieces of their surroundings and use them for their own means.

286

In that slot called data, the reality is sliced in—the junk-shop find, thrift-store clothes, the snippet of James Brown, the stolen paragraph from Proust, and so on.

287

In hip-hop, realness is something to have and express but not question. Realness is sacred. Realness is taboo. Realness refers to a life defined by violence, drugs, cutthroat capitalism—a life not unfamiliar to superstar rappers like The Game (who has been shot five times) and 50 Cent (nine times) when their crews shoot at each other. "I got you stuck off the realness," Prodigy of Mobb Deep raps in the song "Shook Ones Pt. II," probably the most widely quoted use of the term. "We be the infamous / you heard of us / official Queensbridge murderers." It's Mobb Deep's realness that makes you a "shook one"; it's Prodigy's realness that got you stuck. This leads to the term's larger meaning, the meaning Cormega takes, for example, in titling his debut album *The Realness*. There's no title track to explain the term. It's posted at the front of the album like an emblem representing all that follows. The same for Group Home's song "The Realness," in which DJ Premier samples "Shook Ones Pt. II" to isolate the words "the realness" and "comes equipped." Melachi ends his verse by saying he "comes equipped with that Brainsick shit," referring to the guest rappers from the Brainsick Mob, but that's all we know about these terms. There's no definition of realness, only a declaration that they're equipped with it. In the spoken-word introduction to his song "Look in My Eyes," Obie Trice says, "Every man determines his definition of realness, what's real to him." Realness is not reality, something that can be defined or identified. Reality is what is imposed on you; realness is what you impose back. Reality is something you could question; realness is beyond all doubt.

288

Cultural and commercial languages invade us 24/7. That slogan I just heard on the TV commercial: I can't get it out of my head. That melody from the theme song to that syndicated sit-com that arrives at seven every night: we're colonized by this stuff. It invades our lives and our lexicon. This might be of no consequence to the average media consumer, but it spells trouble for the artist. There is now a slogan, a melody, a raw building block of art living in his brain that he doesn't own and can't use.

289

The evolution of copyright law has effectively stunted the development of sampling, thereby protecting the creative property of artists but obstructing the natural evolution of human creativity, which has always possessed cannibalistic tendencies. With copyright laws making the sampling of popular music virtually impossible, a new technique has evolved in which recordings are made that mimic the recordings that the artists would like to sample. These mimic recordings—not nearly as satisfying as sampling the original record—are then sampled and looped in the same way that the original would have been. We don't want a mimic of a piece of music, though; we want the actual piece of music presented through a new lens. Replication isn't reproduction. The copy transcends the original. The original is nothing but a collection of previous cultural movements. All of culture is an appropriation game.

290

People are always talking about originality, but what do they mean? As soon as we are born, the world begins to work upon us, and this goes on to the end. What can we call our own except energy, strength, and will? If I could give an account of all that I owe to great predecessors and contemporaries, there would be but a small balance in my favor.

291

A great man quotes bravely and will not draw on his invention when his memory serves him with a word as good. What he quotes, he fills with his own voice and humor, and the whole cyclopedia of his table talk is presently believed to be his own.

292

Mixtapes are used—as they've traditionally been used—to advertise and promote a new record, but they're also becoming a forum for illegal music: music that has uncleared samples and thus can't be released through proper channels. Much more than a collection of songs, mixtapes have a host who introduces the programs and talks in between songs as if the listener were at a live show. A DJ selects the music and mixes many different songs together into new pieces. Many times the singers from the selected songs will customize the song and add new twists unique to that particular mixtape. The new vocals are often extremely self-reflexive, mentioning the mix-tape itself and how it was made. In the majority of mixtapes I've heard, the original songs are re-presented in unique new ways, but record labels then bust their own promotional oper-atives. Which is similar, in a sense, to the situation regarding file sharing: the companies complaining about downloading (e.g., Sony) are the same companies making the machines that do the downloading. Instead of prosecuting people who have an interest in their product, these companies could try to figure out how to use this consumer interest to their advan-tage. Mass-media producers are wasting their time trying to hold the dam together, but it broke several years ago. The technology to duplicate, copy, and sample mass-produced media isn't going away. What do we do with "outlaw" works of art? If I'm burning copies of *Titanic* and selling them as supposedly real copies of the movie, that seems illegal, but if I use elements of *Titanic* in a *Tarnation*-style film, that doesn't seem wrong to me. I think it should be a question of intent. However, both cases are wrong in the eyes of the law.

293

Chris Moukarbel, who was sued by Paramount Pictures over a twelve-minute video based on a bootleg Oliver Stone film script about 9/11, had another video in a New York gallery exhibition that sought to marry politics and art. This one was created from film shot in the process of making the video that led to the lawsuit. Paramount filed suit in United States District Court in Washington, saying that Mr. Moukarbel's original video, *World Trade Center 2006,* infringed on the copyright of the screenplay for Mr. Stone's $60 million film *World Trade Center.* "I'm interested in memorial and the way Hollywood represents historical events," Mr. Moukarbel said in an interview a month before the Paramount movie was released. "Through their access and budget, they're able to affect a lot of people's ideas about an event and also affect policy. I was deliberately using their script and preempting their release to make a statement about power."

294

The progress of artistic growth in many media is being hindered, like those poor pine trees in alpine zones able to grow only a few weeks each year. For writers and artists who came of age amid mountains and mountains of cultural artifacts and debris: all of this is part of their lives, but much of it is off-limits for artistic expression because someone "owns" it.

295

Shepard Fairey, borrowing liberally from traditions of urban art and the propaganda poster, took an image off Google and transformed it into a major icon of the 2008 campaign. The image (Obama, atop the word *HOPE,* looking skyward and awash in red, white, and blue) condensed the feeling of the Obama campaign into a single visual statement. It wasn't until after the election that the Associated Press realized that it owned the copyright to one of the photos from which Fairey worked. Mannie Garcia, the photographer who took the photo, had no idea it was his work until it was pointed out to him. He later claimed that it was he who actually owned the copyright. This didn't stop the Associated Press from demanding a large sum of money in "damages" for the now famous photo, which—until very recently—it didn't know it had and in fact may not own the copyright to. In 2009, backed by Stanford University's Fair Use Project, Fairey countersued the AP. When Fairey later acknowledged that he had lied about which image he'd used as the basis for his poster, Fairey's attorneys withdrew from the case. Lawrence Lessig, the director of the Edmond J. Safra Foundation Center for Ethics at Harvard, who had been advising Fairey but not representing him, said that the significant issue in fair-use cases is whether the image has been transformed from the original; if it has been "fundamentally transformed," he said, it is protected by copyright law.

296

Most of the passages in this book are taken from other sources. Nearly every passage I've clipped I've also revised, at least a little—for the sake of compression, consistency, or whim. You mix and scratch the shit up to the level your own head is at . . .

297

You'll notice that he doesn't assert ownership over his ideas. He's in some kind of Artaudian condition where all the ideas are unoriginated and unsourced; that's how he can claim anybody else's ideas as his own. Really all he wants to do is acquire everyone's inner life.

298

Stolen property is the soul. Take them out of this book, for instance—you might as well take the book along with them; one cold eternal winter would reign in every page of it. Restore them to the writer: he steps forth like a bridegroom.

299

He dedicated his scruples and his sleepless nights to repeating an already extant book in an alien tongue.

300

The recombinant (the bootleg, the remix, the mash-up) has become the characteristic pivot at the turn of our two centuries. We live at a peculiar juncture, one in which the CD (an object) and the recombinant (a process) still, however briefly, coexist. There seems little doubt, though, as to the direction things are going. The recombinant is manifest in forms as diverse as Alan Moore's graphic novel *The League of Extraordinary Gentlemen,* machinima generated with game engines (*Quake, Halo, World of Warcraft*), Dean Scream remixes, genre-warping fan fiction from the universes of *Star Trek* or *Buffy,* the JarJar-less *Phantom Edit,* brand-hybrid athletic shoes, and Japanese collectibles rescued from anonymity by custom paint jobs. We seldom legislate new technologies into being. They emerge, and we plunge with them into whatever vortices of changes they generate. We legislate after the fact, in a perpetual game of catch-up, as best we can, while our new technologies redefine us—as surely and perhaps as terribly as we've been redefined by television.

k

reality tv

301

The American reality show *Survivor* is derived from the popular Swedish reality show *Expedition Robinson,* which debuted
in Sweden in 1997 and was sold to Mark Burnett in 1998.
Survivor first aired on CBS in 2000 and now has shows in
thirty other countries. *Expedition Robinson* was named after and
loosely based on the Daniel Defoe novel *Robinson Crusoe* (1719),
which was based on the true story of Alexander Selkirk, which
Defoe read in Richard Steele's magazine *The Englishman.*
Selkirk was a sea merchant who pirated for the government
and, citing the dangerous captain and damaged boat as reasons
for not wanting to sail around the Horn of Africa for loot,
asked to be left on an island and rescued five years later. He was
on the island from 1704 until 1709 and grew accustomed
to solitude. In the novel, Crusoe rejects his life as a lawyer
and takes to the sea. His boat is overtaken by pirates, and he
eventually becomes a Brazilian plantation owner. When he
leaves to collect slaves, he's the only survivor of the crash that

maroons him. He builds a home for himself, feeds himself, and (unlike Selkirk) encounters other inhabitants on the island, such as his companion Friday and cannibals. After twenty-eight years, two months, and nineteen days, he's rescued.

302

"This is the true story of seven strangers, picked to live in a house and have their lives taped. Find out what happens when people stop being polite and start getting *real*. *The Real World*!"—the first reality show, although only the first couple of years were "real" (sans orchestration). *Surreal Life:* pretty much the same thing as *The Real World,* but with seven former celebrities (turns out celebrities are real people). The "reality" of contest shows derives from contestants wanting things that people in real life want. The contestants on, for instance, *American Idol, America's Next Top Model,* and *The Apprentice* all want jobs that are nearly impossible to get but remain the goal of many young people: pop singer, model, rock star, and making a million dollars a year working for Donald Trump. The shows usually involve people living in a house with the other hopefuls and then intermittently during the week completing some act of courage or strength to prove they shouldn't be eliminated that week. The models go on modeling shoots in which they're asked, say, to be suspended in the air with wires while wearing superhero outfits or to pose naked except for body paint or to pose in their underwear with male models also in their underwear. On *The Bachelor,* the bachelorettes go on excruciating dates with the prize guy: horseback riding in the snow for those afraid of horses and cold, fencing with a face-enclosing helmet on for the claustrophobic. These moments of "reality" are worse than what most of us experience dating or working, but they're an opportunity for us to watch what someone else would do if things turned really bad, to steel ourselves, perhaps, for the date from hell or for the job that demands we be braver and smarter than we actually are. In *The Biggest Loser,* teams of obese men and women compete to see who can lose the greatest percentage of body weight. The team that loses at each week's weigh-in must send home one person who will no longer have the opportunity to be on TV and work with the trainer to become thin. In *Extreme Makeover,* which lasted four seasons, each week two contestants were provided extensive plastic surgery, dental makeovers, and training sessions. Candidates would write in about how being ugly by society's standards had hampered their lives. Two of the worst cases were selected and sent to LA to live and consult specialists. The show followed the two contestants through their various surgeries and ended with the "unveiling" in front of their family and friends, who were often moved to tears. I often found myself musing that these people had way more friends than I do. *The Swan,* canceled after only two seasons (too painful): a handful of "ugly ducklings" competed to become the one most transformed (by, principally, plastic surgeries) and named by judges as the swan. *Last Comic Standing:* two judges left the show when they realized that their votes meant nothing, that the producers determined who won each week; the show survived the scandal. *The Contender:* sixteen semipro boxers duked it out; one of the losers killed himself. In 2008, a 2005 contestant from *American Idol* committed suicide in front of Paula Abdul's house. *Rock Star INXS:* INXS auditioned singers to replace their lead singer, Michael Hutchence, who killed himself in 1997. *Hit Me Baby One More Time:* 1980s one-hit wonders attempted comebacks (no one was interested).

303

In 2008, more votes were cast for *American Idol* than for Barack Obama for president: 97 million for *American Idol* and, on Election Day, 70 million for Obama.

304

I try not to watch reality TV, but it happens anyway. My aunt and uncle, both of whom are pretty intellectual, live two doors down from me and watch reality TV, so I watch it with them sometimes (they like Donald Trump's show and *Project Runway*). My wife (another very intelligent person) also watches *America's Next Top Model,* so I'm all too familiar with that show as well. I think different people get sucked into reality shows for different reasons. My aunt and uncle seem to like the competition aspect. It becomes a blurry vision of televised sports (which also has that added sense of immediacy because it's unfiltered, is "really" happening, and therefore there's the feeling that in the next minute anything can happen—which adds to the excitement of a competition). My wife seems to like *America's Next Top Model* for the elements you would find in a soap opera: the intrigue and fighting among the contestants. The producers have a way of typecasting and highlighting aspects of each girl's personality for greater effect (nearly everyone wants to see beautiful young women gossip and argue). There's also always at least one minor subplot. However scripted the show is, it's more compelling than standard soap operas. I like to see how reality shows are put together, especially the way in which the shows are a hybrid mutant of documentaries, game shows, and soaps. The producers have no problem blurring the lines between these three types of shows: they take what works and discard the rest.

305

My big-picture philosophy is that with shows like this, I don't think our viewers necessarily differentiate between what's scripted and what's not. Our primary goal is to make a show that's compelling.

306

Readers thirst for a narrative, any narrative, and will turn to the most compelling one.

307

There's no longer any such thing as fiction or nonfiction; there's only narrative. (Is there even narrative?)

308

Bored with the airbrushed perfection of *Friends,* we want to watch real people stuck on tropical islands without dental floss. We want our viewing to reflect our complicated, messy, difficult, overloaded, overstimulated lives. Let's see messy houses getting clean, bratty children caught on hidden cameras, actual arguments between genuine young people being authentically solipsistic.

309

In *Jacob's Room,* Virginia Woolf describes the dilemma of Charles Steele, who's painting a still-life portrait: a cloud drifts into view, Mrs. Flanders's sons run around the beach, she grows upset about the letter she's writing, and she won't stop moving. If Charles instructs Mrs. Flanders to stop moving, he's altering the world in order for it to match what he wants to paint, rather than shaping his painting to reflect what's actually occurring in the world.

310

The bachelorette on the brink of true love with one of several men she has known for seven hours; the cad who manipulates his beloved on cue—two narratives: false actualization and authentic shame. The success of the genre reflects our lust for emotional meaning. We really do want to feel, even if that means indulging in someone else's joy or woe. We have a thirst for reality (other people's reality, edited) even as we suffer a surfeit of reality (our own—boring/painful).

311

Forms serve the culture; when they die, they die for a good reason: they're no longer embodying what it's like to be alive. If reality TV manages to convey something that a more manifestly scripted and plotted show doesn't, that's less an affront to writers than a challenge.

1

collage

312

I am quite content to go down to posterity as a scissors-and-paste man.

313

If you grow up not with toys bought in the shop but things that are found around the farm, you do a sort of bricolage. Bits of string and wood. Making all sorts of things, like webs across the legs of a chair. And then you sit there, like the spider. The urge to connect bits that don't seem to belong together has fascinated me all my life.

314

Collage is a demonstration of the many becoming the one, with the one never fully resolved because of the many that continue to impinge upon it.

315

While we tend to conceive of the operations of the mind as unified and transparent, they're actually chaotic and opaque. There's no invisible boss in the brain, no central meaner, no unitary self in command of our activities and utterances. There's no internal spectator of a Cartesian theater in our heads to applaud the march of consciousness across its stage.

316

Collage's parts always seem to be competing for a place in some unfinished scene.

317

The law of mosaics: how to deal with parts in the absence of wholes.

318

Resolution and conclusion are inherent in a plot-driven narrative.

319

Conventional fiction teaches the reader that life is a coherent, fathomable whole that concludes in neatly wrapped-up revelation. Life, though—standing on a street corner, channel surfing, trying to navigate the web or a declining relationship, hearing that a close friend died last night—flies at us in bright splinters.

320

Coleridge conceives God's creation to be a continuing process, which has an analogy in the creative perception (primary imagination) of all human minds. The creative process is repeated, or "echoed," on still a third level by the "secondary imagination" of the poet, which dissolves the products of primary perception in order to shape them into a new and unified creation—the imaginative passage or poem. "Fancy," on the other hand, can only manipulate "fixities and definites" that, linked by association, come to it ready-made from perception. Its products, therefore, are not re-creations (echoes of God's original creative process) but mosaic-like reassemblies of existing bits and pieces.

321

Story seems to say that everything happens for a reason, and I want to say, *No, it doesn't.*

322

If I'm reading a book and it seems truly interesting, I tend to start reading back to front in order not to be too deeply under the sway of progress.

323

I have a narrative, but you will be put to it to find it.

324

The absence of plot leaves the reader room to think about other things.

325

With relatively few exceptions, the novel sacrifices too much, for me, on the altar of plot.

326

Plots are for dead people.

327

The novel is dead. Long live the antinovel, built from scraps.

328

I'm not interested in collage as the refuge of the composition-ally disabled. I'm interested in collage as (to be honest) an evolution beyond narrative.

329

All definitions of montage have a common denominator; they all imply that meaning is not inherent in any one shot but is created by the juxtaposition of shots. Lev Kuleshov, an early Russian filmmaker, intercut images of an actor's expressionless face with images of a bowl of soup, a woman in a coffin, and a child with a toy. Viewers of the film praised the actor's performance; they saw in his face (emotionless as it was) hunger, grief, and affection. They saw, in other words, what was not really there in the separate images. Meaning and emotion were created not by the content of the individual images but by the relationship of the images to one another.

330

Everything I write, I believe instinctively, is to some extent collage. Meaning, ultimately, is a matter of adjacent data.

331

Renata Adler's collage novel *Speedboat* captivates by its jagged and frenetic changes of pitch and tone and voice. She confides, reflects, tells a story, aphorizes, undercuts the aphorism, then undercuts that. If she's cryptic in one paragraph, she's clear in the next. She changes subjects like a brilliant schizophrenic, making irrational sense. She's intimate: bed talk uninhibited by conventions. Ideas, experiences, and emotions are inseparable. I don't know what she'll say next. She tantalizes by being simultaneously daring and elusive. The book builds: images recur, ideas are interwoven, names reappear. Paragraphs are miniature stories. She's always present, teasing things apart, but not from a distance. There's very little that's abstract. I can feel her breathe. "The point has never quite been entrusted to me," she says, and so we must keep reading, for we know there will be another way of looking at everything. In many ways the book has suspense and momentum. She's promising us something; something is around the corner. How long can she go on this way? I don't know, but timing is everything. She has to quit before we do and still give an oblique, sly sense of closure, of satisfaction. You can see her working hard on that in the last paragraph.

332
A great painting comes together, just barely.

333
A mosaic, made out of broken dishes, makes no attempt to hide the fact that it's made out of broken dishes, in fact flaunts it.

334
Momentum, in literary mosaic, derives not from narrative but from the subtle, progressive buildup of thematic resonances.

335
I look at melody as rhythm.

336
All art constantly aspires toward the condition of music.

337

I wanted my first novel to be a veritable infarct of narrative cloggers—the trick being to feel your way through each clog by blowing it up until its obstructiveness finally reveals not blank mass but unlooked-for seepage points of passage.

338

—the shapely swirl of energy holding shattered fragments in place, but only just.

339

Collage is pieces of other things. Their edges don't meet.

340

Found objects, chance creations, ready-mades (mass-produced items promoted into art objects, such as Duchamp's "Fountain"—urinal as sculpture) abolish the separation between art and life. The commonplace is miraculous if rightly seen.

341

You don't make art; you find it.

342

The main question collage artists face: you've found some interesting material—how do you go about arranging it?

343

The question isn't *What do you look at?* but *What do you see?*

344

—plunged into a world of complete happiness in which every triviality becomes imbued with significance.

345

—the singular obsessions endlessly revised.

346

The task is not primarily to "think up" a story, but to penetrate the story, to discard the elements of it that are merely shell, or husk, and that give apparent form to the story but actually obscure its essence. In other words, the problem is to transcend the givens of a narrative.

347

I love literature, but not because I love stories per se. I find nearly all the moves the traditional novel makes unbelievably predictable, tired, contrived, and essentially purposeless. I can never remember characters' names, plot developments, lines of dialogue, details of setting. It's not clear to me what such narratives are supposedly revealing about the human condition. I'm drawn to literature instead as a form of thinking, consciousness, wisdom-seeking. I like work that's focused not only page by page but line by line on what the writer really cares about as opposed to work that assumes that what the writer cares about will magically creep through the cracks of narrative, which is the way I experience most stories and novels. Collage works are nearly always "about what they're about"— which may sound a tad tautological—but when I read a book that I really love, I'm excited because I can feel the writer's excitement that in every paragraph he's manifestly exploring his subject.

348

As a moon rocket ascends, different stages of the engine do what they must to accelerate the capsule. Each stage of the engine is jettisoned until only the capsule is left with the astronauts on its way to the moon. In linear fiction, the whole structure is accelerating toward the epiphanic moment, and certainly the parts are necessary for the final experience, but I still feel that the writer and the reader can jettison the pages leading to the epiphany. They serve a purpose and then fall into the Pacific Ocean, so I'm left with Gabriel Conroy and his falling faintly, faintly falling, and I'm heading to the moon in the capsule, but the rest of the story has fallen away. In collage, every fragment is a capsule: I'm on my way to the moon on every page.

349

The very nature of collage demands fragmented materials, or at least materials yanked out of context. Collage is, in a way, only an accentuated act of editing: picking through options and presenting a new arrangement (albeit one that, due to its variegated source material, can't be edited into the smooth, traditional whole that a work of complete fiction could be). The act of editing may be the key postmodern artistic instrument.

350

Thomas Jefferson went through the New Testament and removed all the miracles, leaving only the teachings. Take a source, extract what appeals to you, discard the rest. Such an act of editorship is bound to reflect something of the individual doing the editing: a plaster cast of an aesthetic—not the actual thing, but the imprint of it.

351

—the transformation, through framing, of outtakes into totems.

352

This project must raise the art of quoting without quotation marks to the very highest level. Its theory is intimately linked to that of montage.

353

I hate quotations.

354

In collage, writing is stripped of the pretense of originality and appears as a practice of mediation, of selection and contextualization, a practice, almost, of reading.

355

Our debt to tradition through reading and conversation is so massive, our protest so rare and insignificant—and this commonly on the ground of other reading and hearing—that in large sense, one would say there is no pure originality. All minds quote. Old and new make the warp and woof of every moment. There is no thread that is not a twist of these two strands. By necessity, by proclivity, and by delight, we all quote. It is as difficult to appropriate the thoughts of others as it is to invent.

356

Our country, customs, laws, our ambitions, and our notions of fit and fair—all these we never made; we found them ready-made; we but quote from them. What would remain to me if this art of appropriation were derogatory to genius? Every one of my writings has been furnished to me by a thousand different persons, a thousand things; wise and foolish have brought me, without suspecting it, the offering of their thoughts, faculties, and experience. My work is an aggregation of beings taken from the whole of nature. It bears the name of Goethe.

357

There are two kinds of filmmaking: Hitchcock's (the film is complete in the director's mind) and Coppola's (which thrives on process). For Hitchcock, any variation from the complete internal idea is seen as a defect. The perfection already exists. Coppola's approach is to harvest the random elements that the process throws up, things that were not in his mind when he began.

358

The usual reproach against the essay, that it is fragmentary and random, itself assumes the givenness of totality and suggests that man is in control of this totality. The desire of the essay, though, is not to filter the eternal out of the transitory; it wants, rather, to make the transitory eternal.

359

Nonlinear. Discontinuous. Collage-like. An assemblage. As is already more than self-evident.

360

The problem of scale is interesting. How long will the reader stay engaged? I don't mean stay dutifully but stay charmed, seduced, and beguiled. Robbe-Grillet's *Ghosts in the Mirror*, which he calls a romanesque, is a quasi-memoir with philosophical reflections, intimate flashes, and personal addresses to the reader. About this length, I think: 174 pages.

361

You don't need a story. The question is *How long do you not need a story?*

362

Nothing is going to happen in this book.

363

The purpose of art is to impart the sensation of things as they are perceived and not as they are known. Art exists that one may recover the sensation of life; it exists to make one feel things, to make the stone stony.

364

By incorporating materials that are inextricably linked to the realities of daily life, the collage artist establishes an immediate identification, both real and imagined, between the viewer and the work of art.

365

It may be that nowadays in order to move us, abstract pictures need, if not humor, then at least some admission of their own absurdity—expressed in genuine awkwardness, or in an authentic disorder.

366

Any opportunity that a writer has to engage the reader intimately in the act of creating the text is an opportunity to grab on to. White space does that. I don't ever want to be bored, and I certainly don't ever want any of my readers to be bored. I'd much rather risk them getting annoyed and frustrated than bored.

367

The gaps between paragraphs = the gaps between people (content tests form).

368

These fragments I have shored against my ruins. Cyril Connolly's *The Unquiet Grave*. Eduardo Galeano's *The Book of Embraces*. Richard Brautigan's *Trout Fishing in America*. Sven Lindqvist's *A History of Bombing*.

369

The grandfather clock is the reflection of its historical period, when time was orderly and slow. *Tick-tock. Tick-tock. Ticktock*. It stood there in the front hall in its great, carven case, with a pendulum like the sun or the moon. There was something monumental and solid about time. By the 1930s and '40s, wristwatches were neurotic and talked very fast— *tick-tick-tick-tick*—with a second hand going around. Next, we had liquid-crystal watches that didn't show any time at all until you pressed a button. When you took your finger off, time disappeared. Now, no one wears a watch; your phone has the time.

370

If fiction has a main theme, a primary character, an occupation, a methodology, a criterion, a standard, a purpose (is there anything left for fiction to have?), it is time itself. One basic meaning of narrative: to create time where there was none. A fiction writer who tells stories is a maker of time. Not liking a story might be akin to not believing in its depiction of time. To the writer searching for the obstacle to surpass, time would look plenty worthy a hurdle. If something must be overcome, ruined, subverted in order for fiction to stay matterful (yes, maybe the metaphor of progress in literary art is pretentious and tired *at this point* (there's time again, aging what was once such a fine idea)), then time would be the thing to beat, the thing fiction seemingly cannot do without and, therefore, to grow or change, must. Time must die.

371

Nonfiction, qua label, is nothing more or less than a very flexible (easily breakable) frame that allows you to pull the thing away from narrative and toward contemplation, which is all I've ever wanted.

372

Stephen Dobyns says that every lyric poem implies a narrative, but the lyric poet might just as easily reply that every narrative poem obscures a lyric. The man in the restaurant crushing a wineglass in his hand acts out an emotional complex not wholly explained by a hard day at the office, or being cheated in the taxi, or what his companion just said. If the narrative writer is instinctively curious about the individuating "story," the distinct sequence of events preceding that broken glass, the lyric poet may be as naturally drawn to the isolated human moment of frustration—the distilled, indelible peak on the emotional chart.

373

In *Moulin Rouge,* Baz Luhrmann takes the most thrilling moments in a movie musical—the seconds before the actors are about to burst into song and dance, when every breath they take is heightened—and makes an entire picture of such pinnacles.

374

When plot shapes a narrative, it's like knitting a scarf. You have this long piece of string and many choices about how to knit, but you understand that a sequence is involved, a beginning and an end, with one part of the weave very logically and sequentially connected to the next. You can figure out where the beginning is and where the last stitch is cast off. Webs look orderly, too, but unless you watch the spider weaving, you'll never know where it started. It could be attached to branches or table legs or eaves in six or eight places. You won't know the sequence in which the different cells were spun and attached to one another. You have to decide for yourself how to read its patterning, but if you pluck it at any point, the entire web will vibrate.

m

in praise
of brevity

375

The short-short story isn't a new form. It's not as if, in 1974, there sprung from the head of Zeus the short-short story. Still, the short-short (dreadful label, but what's better?) feels particularly relevant to contemporary life. Delivering only highlights and no downtime, the short-short seems to me to gain access to contemporary feeling states more effectively than the conventional story does. As rap, movie trailers, stand-up comedy, fast food, commercials, sound bites, phone sex, bumper stickers, email, voice mail, and *Headline News* all do, short-shorts cut to the chase. Short-shorts eschew the furniture-moving, the table-setting typical of the longer story. *Here, in a page or a page and a half, I'll attempt to unveil for you my vision of life;* short-shorts are often thrillingly nervous-making for both writer and reader. In the best short-shorts, the writer seems to have miraculously figured out a way to stage, in a very compressed space, his own metaphysic: *Life feels like this* or at least *Some aspect of life feels like this.* What in the traditional story requires character and plot is, in the short-short, supplanted by theme and idea.

Every work, no matter how short or antilinear, needs momentum; the momentum of the short-short is lyrical in nature—
What does this mean?—rather than narrative in nature: *What
happens next?* My reaction to a lot of longer stories is often
Remind me again why I read this, or *The point being?* The point,
such as it is, often seems to me woefully or willfully obscure in
even the most well-made stories. I've become an impatient
writer and reader: I seem to want the moral, psychological,
philosophical news to be delivered *now,* and this (the rapid
emotional-delivery system) is something that the short-short
can do exceedingly well. Even as they're exploring extremely
serious and complex material, short-short writers frequently
use a certain mock modesty to give the work a tossed-off tone
and disarm the reader. The reader thinks he's reading a diary
entry, when in fact it's a lyric essay or prose poem. Short-shorts
remind me of algebraic equations or geometry proofs or lab
experiments or jigsaw puzzles or carom shots or very cruel
jokes. They're magic tricks, with meaning. Examples: Jayne
Anne Phillips's "Sweethearts," Jerome Stern's "Morning
News," Any Hempel's "In the Animal Shelter," Linda Brewer's
"20/20," Gregory Burnham's "Subtotals."

376

The merit of style exists precisely in that it delivers the greatest number of ideas in the fewest number of words.

377

How much can one remove and still have the composition be
intelligible? This understanding, or its lack, divides those who
can write from those who can really write. Chekhov removed
the plot. Pinter, elaborating, removed the history, the narration; Beckett, the characterization. We hear it anyway. Omission is a form of creation.

378

The Canterbury Tales, a compendium of all the good yarns Chaucer knew, has lasted centuries, while the long-winded medieval narratives went into museums.

379

As Stephen Frears, the director of *High Fidelity,* worked to translate the best moments of the Nick Hornby novel on which the movie was based, he found to his surprise that the best moments were the voice-overs, especially the direct speeches of Rob Gordon (John Cusack) to the camera. Frears said, "What we realized was that the novel was a machine to get to twelve crucial speeches in the book about romance and art and music and list-making and masculine distance and the masculine drive for art and the masculine difficulty with intimacy." This is the case for most novels: you have to read seven hundred pages to get the handful of insights that were the reason the book was written, and the apparatus of the novel is there as a huge, elaborate, overbuilt stage set.

380

I'm a third of the way through Thomas Bernhard's *The Loser,* and at first I was excited by it, but now I'm a little bored. I may not finish it.

It's so beautiful and so pessimistic.

Yes, but it doesn't hold one's interest the way a nineteenth-century novel does. I'm never bored when I'm reading George Eliot or Tolstoy.

I am.

And you're not bored when you're reading Bernhard?

I'm bored by plot. I'm bored when it's all written out, when there isn't any shorthand.

381

In order to make it easier to handle, Darwin would cut a large book in half; he'd also tear out any chapters he didn't find of interest.

382

The line of beauty is the line of perfect economy.

383

It is my ambition to say in ten sentences what everyone else says in a whole book—what everyone else does not say in a whole book.

n

genre

384

The lyric essay doesn't expound, is suggestive rather than exhaustive, depends on gaps, may merely mention. It might move by association, leaping from one path of thought to another by way of imagery or connotation, advancing by juxtaposition or sidewinding poetic logic. It often accretes by fragments, taking shape mosaically, its import visible only when one stands back and sees it whole. It partakes of the poem in its density and shapeliness, its distillation of ideas and musicality of language, and partakes of the essay in its weight, its overt desire to engage with facts, melding its allegiance to the actual with its passion for imaginative form. It gives primacy to artfulness over the conveying of information, forsaking narrative line, discursiveness, and the art of persuasion in favor of idiosyncratic meditation. Generally, it's short, concise, and punchy, like a prose poem. It may, though, meander, making use of other genres when they serve its purpose, sampling the techniques of fiction, drama, journalism, song, and film. The stories it tells may be no more than metaphors. Or, storyless, it may spiral in on itself, circling the core of a single image or idea, without climax, without a paraphrasable theme. It stalks its subject but isn't content to merely explain or confess. Loyal to that original sense of "essay" as a test or a quest, an attempt at making sense, the lyric essay sets off on an uncharted course through interlocking webs of idea, circumstance, and language—a pursuit with no foreknown conclusion, an arrival that might still leave the writer questioning. While it's ruminative, it leaves pieces of experience undigested and tacit, inviting the reader's participatory interpretation. Its voice, spoken from a privacy that we overhear and enter, has the intimacy we've come to expect in the personal essay, yet in the lyric essay the voice is often more reticent, almost coy, aware of the compliment it pays the reader by dint of understatement. Perhaps we're drawn to the lyric now because it seems less possible and rewarding to approach the world through the front door, through the myth of objectivity. Similitude often seems more revealing than verisimilitude. We turn to the writer to reconcoct meaning from the bombardments of experience: to shock, thrill, still the racket, and tether our attention.

385

The roominess of the term *nonfiction:* an entire dresser labeled *nonsocks.*

386

"Essay" is a verb, not just a noun; "essaying" is a process.

387

Essay: theater of the brain.

388

Emotion evolves into analysis.

Public life spills over into personal anecdote.

Sensations are felt as argument.

Argument is conveyed as sensation.

Opinions erupt into ideas.

In essays, ideas are the protagonists.

389

The reader of biography and autobiography (and history and journalism) is always and everywhere dogged by epistemological insecurity. In a work of nonfiction we almost never know the truth of what happened. The ideal of unmediated reporting is regularly achieved only in fiction, where the writer faithfully reports on what's going on in his imagination. When James reports in *The Golden Bowl* that the Prince and Charlotte are sleeping together, we have no reason to doubt him or to wonder whether Maggie is "overreacting" to what she's seeing. James's report is a true report. The facts of imaginative literature are as hard as the rock that Samuel Johnson kicked when, asked how he would refute Bishop Berkeley's notion that matter doesn't exist, he struck "his foot with mighty force against a large stone, till he rebounded from it, and said, 'I refute it thus.' " We must always take the novelist's and the playwright's and the poet's word, just as we're almost always free to doubt the biographer's or the autobiographer's or the historian's or the journalist's. In imaginative literature we're always constrained from considering alternative scenarios; there are none. This is the way it *is*. Only in nonfiction does the question of what happened and how people thought and felt remain open.

390

True essayists rarely write novels. Essayists are a species of metaphysician: they're inquisitive and analytic about the least grain of being. Novelists go about the strenuous business of marrying and burying their people, or else they send them to sea or to Africa or at least out of town. Essayists in their stillness ponder love and death. Only inner space—interesting, active, significant—can conceive the contemplative essay. Essays, unlike novels, emerge from the sensations of the self. Fiction creeps into foreign bodies: the novelist can inhabit not only a sex not his own but also beetles and noses and hunger artists and nomads and beasts. The essay is personal.

391

A conversational dynamic—the desire for contact—is ingrained in the form.

392

It is Sir Thomas Browne's introspection that shifted us from the outside world of rhetoric to the inner world of mystery and wonder.

393

My picturing will, by definition, distort its subject; it's a record and an embodiment of a process of knowing; it's about the making of knowledge, which is a much larger and more unstable thing than the marshaling of facts.

394

The memoir rightly belongs to the imaginative world, and once writers and readers make their peace with this, there will be less argument over the questions regarding the memoir's relation to the "facts" and "truth."

395

What does it matter if Frey actually spent the few nights in prison he writes about in his book? Fake jail time was merely a device to get a point across, a plausible situation in which to frame his suffering.

396

The real kinship among genres today is less between the memoir and the novel and more between memoir and poetry. We make a mistake in thinking of memoir as nonfiction. It's really nonpoetry. I don't think we can understand the strong impulse of the memoir if we look only to fiction for its roots.

397

When a lyric poet uses, characteristically, the first-person voice, we don't say accusingly, *But did this really happen the way you say it did?* We accept the honest and probably inevitable mixture of mind and spirit. The reason we don't interrogate poetry as we do memoir is that we have a long and pretty sophisticated history of how to read the poetic voice. We accept that its task is to find emotional truth within experience, so we aren't all worked up about the literal. We don't yet have that history or tradition with memoir. We persist in seeing the genre as a summing up of life, even though that's not typically how the genre is used in the great rash of memoirs that have been published in the past twenty years or so. When we house memoir under the umbrella of nonfiction, we take the word "nonfiction" very seriously. We act astonished, even dismayed, when we find out that the memoiristic voice is doing something other than putting down facts. We know that's not the case, but we're constantly struggling with this inevitability as if with the transgressions of a recidivist pedophile. We need to see the genre in poetic terms.

O

contradiction

398
This sentence is a lie.

399
Something can be true and untrue at the same time.

400
The whole content of my being shrieks in contradiction against myself.

401
"The test of a first-rate intelligence is the ability to hold two opposed ideas in the mind at the same time, and still retain the ability to function." I've always disliked the unnecessary comma in the middle of this famous Fitzgerald dictum, suggestive as it is of an inability to hold two opposed ideas in the mind at the same time while still retaining etc.

402

We are, I know not how, double within ourselves, with the result that we do not believe what we believe, and we cannot rid ourselves of what we condemn.

403

Negative capability: capable of being in uncertainties, mysteries, doubts, without any irritable reaching after fact and reason.

404

It's natural to enter into dialogues and disputes with others, because it's natural to enter into disputes with oneself: the mind works by contradiction.

405

Great art is clear thinking about mixed feelings.

406

One of the tricks in writing a personal essay is that you have to develop a dialogue between the parts of yourself that in a way corresponds to the conflict in fiction. You cop to various tendencies, and then you struggle with these tendencies.

407

Ambitious work doesn't resolve contradictions in a spurious harmony but instead embodies the contradictions, pure and uncompromised, in its innermost structure.

408

One view is "There's something in charge and I wanna get straight with it." Another view is "There's something in charge and it means me no good and I wanna get the fuck out of here." And the third is "There's nothing and everything going on." The third, because it contains the other two, is most appealing to me.

doubt

409

Why bother conducting an experiment at all if you know what results it will yield? Maybe every essay automatically is in some way experimental—not an outline traveling toward a foregone conclusion but an unmapped quest that has sprung from the word *question.* I don't know where the journey ends; otherwise, why call this action *journey*?

410

There is something heroic in the essayist's gesture of striking out toward the unknown, not only without a map but without certainty that there is anything worthy to be found.

411

We're only certain ("certain only"?) about what we don't understand.

412

Authenticity comes from a single faithfulness: that to the ambiguity of experience.

413

Maybe the essay is just a conditional form of literature—less a genre in its own right than an attitude that's assumed amid another genre, or the means by which other genres speak to one another.

414

To think with any seriousness is to doubt. Thought is indistinguishable from doubt. To be alive is to be uncertain. I'll take doubt. The essayist argues with himself, and the essayist argues with the reader. The essay enacts doubt; it embodies it as a genre. The very purpose of the genre is to provide a vehicle for essaying.

415

The real story isn't the official story; the real story is my version (wrong, too, but aware that it's wrong) of the official story.

416

Not only is life mostly failure, but in one's failure or pettiness or wrongness exists the living drama of the self.

417

The perpetual aura of doubt is what gives his monologue its authenticity.

418

When we are not sure, we are alive.

q
thinking

419

The world exists. Why re-create it? I want to think about it, try to understand it. What I am is a wisdom junkie, knowing all along that wisdom is, in many ways, junk. I want a literature built entirely out of contemplation and revelation. Who cares about anything else?

420

"The only end of writing is to enable the reader better to enjoy life, or better to endure it"—so goeth the Samuel Johnson dictum; I most admire those books that not only enable me to endure life but show me how they got there. Serious plumbing of consciousness, not flashing of narrative legerdemain, helps me understand another human being. The former is boring in a good sense; the latter is boring in a bad sense. Not *The world is boring; I want to escape it* but *The world is fascinating; I want to investigate it.*

421

I don't know what it's like inside you and you don't know what it's like inside me. A great book allows me to leap over that wall: in a deep, significant conversation with another consciousness, I feel human and unalone.

422

I bear in my hands the disguise by which I conceal my life. A web of meaningless events, I dye it with the magic of my point of view.

423

No artist tolerates reality.

424

If I had the slightest grasp upon my own faculties, I would not make essays. I would make decisions.

425

Is there a sense in which a writer's vision gets more thoroughly and beautifully tested in a book of linked stories than it does in a collection of miscellaneous stories or in a novel? How do linked-story collections combine the capaciousness of novels with the density and intensity of stories? Why do linked stories often have a stronger thematic pull than novels? How does each story in a collection of linked stories achieve closure-but-not-closure? What's the difference between repetition and reprise? To what degree do linked stories seem to be about pattern, about authorial obsession, about watching a writer work and rework his material until he simply has nothing more to say about it? What epistemological questions thus get raised? What ontological questions thus get raised? For example, is everything we know provisional? I'm thinking of Lermontov's

A Hero of Our Time, Kundera's *The Book of Laughter and Forget-ting,* Denis Johnson's *Jesus' Son.*

426

How can I tell what I think until I see what I say?

427

I write entirely to find out what I'm thinking, what I'm look-ing at, what I see, and what it means.

428

The opening sentence of Nabokov's autobiography, *Speak, Memory,* is communal, contemplative: "The cradle rocks above an abyss, and common sense tells us that our existence is but a brief crack of light between two eternities of darkness." By contrast, the first line of his first English-language novel, *The Real Life of Sebastian Knight*—"Sebastian Knight was born on the thirty-first of December 1899, in the former capital of my country"—is concerned with the names, dates, and places of the world. Although *Speak, Memory* is chronological, it is in a sense unplotted, shifting from one character or one city to another not on the basis of narrative but the associations of memory. In *The Real Life of Sebastian Knight,* the transition from place to place is accomplished according to the demands of, especially, temporal progression; most chapters open with a jump forward in time. No matter how traditional or experi-mental a novel may be, the reader is meant to be struck by its fulfillment or frustration of story; we expect autobiography, on the other hand, to be an examination of the process by which it, and its author, came to be. It's easier for autobiography to be about itself than it is for fiction, because by its very definition, autobiography is concerned with the consciousness of its creator in the process of creating himself. If the novelist can deflect through invention the fact that "our existence is but a brief crack of light between two eternities of darkness," the autobiographer is allowed and even expected to surrender to the unfathomable phenomenon that is his own life.

429
Life consists in what a man is thinking of all day.

430
The essayist gives you his thoughts and lets you know, in addition, how he came by them.

431
The glory of the essayist is to tell, once and for all, everything that he or she thinks, knows, and understands.

432
Serious writing actually tries to get somewhere—to make intellectual, emotional, psychic, and philosophical "progress." (This progress could, of course, also be regress.) Obviously, with some very accomplished novelists one feels this via magisterial storytelling (actually, I can think of very few at the moment), but in the work of my favorite writers, the armature of overt drama is dispensed with, and we're left with a deeper drama, the real drama: an active human consciousness trying to figure out how he or she has solved or not solved being alive.

433
Somebody wrote that what I was doing in a certain song was asking a question and then answering the question. That's what I think telling a story is: resolving a thought.

434

—not what happens, but what we're thinking about while nothing, or very little, is happening. The sound of a person sitting alone in the dark, thinking. Hawthorne, "Custom-House." Borges, *Other Inquisitions.* Stendhal, *Maxims on Love.* Baldwin, the early essays. The sound of one hand clapping.

435

The essential tension of serious essay is the ambivalence of the author-narrator toward a given subject. I find this a more compelling way to talk about being alive than through the surrogate selves of fiction. I remember in college telling my girlfriend that I wanted to forge a form that would house only epiphanies—such presumption!—but now, thirty-plus years later, I feel as if I've stumbled onto something approximating that. I want the overt meditation that yields understanding, as opposed to a lengthy narrative that yields—what?—I suppose a sort of extended readerly interest in what happens next.

436

When Nicholson Baker lived in Berkeley for several years (he now lives in Maine), I contrived to think of him as being related to a group of West Coast writers whose interestingness derives for me principally from the ways in which they process information and write about how they process information (to name but a few, Douglas Coupland, Sallie Tisdale, Bernard Cooper, the late David Foster Wallace, Jonathan Raban, Dave Eggers, William T. Vollmann). The West Coast seems somehow to give people the freedom to focus on information and its conduits, its messengers; the East Coast, by contrast, is still to me so much about the old-fashioned minutiae of social strata.

437

What the lyric essay gives you—what fiction doesn't, usually—is the freedom to emphasize its aboutness, its metaphysical meaningfulness. There's plenty of drama, but it's subservient to the larger drama of mind.

438

Maybe the essay really is just a philosophical investigation; maybe, because it's masked by other forms such as story or memoir or lyric or fable, we ignore its most basic form.

439

The motor of fiction is narrative.
The motor of essay is thought.
The default of fiction is storytelling.
The default of essay is memoir.
Fiction: no ideas but in things.
(Serious) essay (what I want): not the thing itself but ideas about the thing.

440

Someone once said to me, quoting someone or other, "Discursive thought is not fiction's most efficient tool; the interaction of characters is everything." This is when I knew I wasn't a fiction writer, because discursive thought is what I read and write for.

441

My daughter, sick, at six: "My thinker isn't thinking."

442

Freud (declining drugs to alleviate pain caused by cancer of the jaw): "I prefer thinking in torment to not being able to think clearly."

443

I hate the inner life.
I'm tired of the thoughts I steer by.

444

There's always a recursive component to utterance (repetition deprives a last stand of its dramatic force).

445

—the chronic American belief that there exists an opposition between reality and mind and one must enlist oneself in the party of reality.

446

American intellectuals, when they're being consciously American or political, are remarkably quick to suggest that an art marked by perception and knowledge, although all very well in its way, can never get us through gross dangers and difficulties.

447

What I love: the critical intelligence in the imaginative position—D. H. Lawrence, *Studies in Classic American Literature;* Wayne Koestenbaum, *The Queen's Throat;* Nicholson Baker, *U & I;* Geoff Dyer, *Out of Sheer Rage;* Terry Castle, "My Heroin Christmas"; Anne Carson, *Eros the Bittersweet;* Roland Barthes, *S/Z;* Nabokov, *Gogol;* Beckett, *Proust;* Proust, all;

William James, *Varieties of Religious Experience*. Sister Mary Ignatius, in other words, explaining it all for you—*les belles dames sans merci:* Joan Didion, all the essays; Pauline Kael, pretty much everything; Elizabeth Hardwick, *Sleepless Nights*.

448

The composition of vast books is a laborious and impoverishing extravagance. To go on for five hundred pages developing an idea whose perfect oral exposition is possible in a few minutes! A better course of procedure is to pretend that these books already exist and then offer a résumé, a commentary.

449

A student in my class, feeling self-conscious about being much older than the other students, told me that he'd been in prison. I asked him what crime he'd committed, and he said, "Shot a dude." He wrote a series of very good but very stoic stories about prison life, and when I asked him why the stories were so tight-lipped, he explained to me the jailhouse concept of "doing your own time," which means that when you're a prisoner you're expected not to burden the other prisoners by complaining about your incarceration or regretting what you had done or, especially, claiming you hadn't done it. "Do your own time": a seductive slogan. I find that I quote it to myself frequently, but really I don't subscribe to the sentiment. I'm not, after all, in prison. Stoicism bores me. What I ultimately believe in is talking about everything until you're blue in the face.

450

Whether we're young, or we're all grown up and just starting out, or we're getting old, or getting so old there's not much time left, we're looking for company, and we're looking for understanding: someone who reminds us that we're not alone, and someone who wonders out loud about things that happen in this life, the way we do when we're walking or sitting or driving, and thinking things over.

451

The right voice can reveal what it's like to be thinking: the inner life in its historical moment.

452

He then learns that in going down into the secrets of his own mind he has descended into the secrets of all minds.

453

In every work of genius we recognize our own rejected thoughts; they come back to us with a certain alienated majesty. Pascal. Rousseau. Nietzsche. Cioran.

454

We don't come to thoughts; they come to us.

455

Hamlet, dying, says, "If I had the time, I would tell you all." The entire play is the Hamlet Show, functioning as a vehicle for Hamlet to give his opinion on everything and anything, as Nietzsche does in *Thus Spoke Zarathustra.* The play could easily be broken up into little sections with headings like "Hamlet on Friendship," "Hamlet on Sexual Fidelity," "Hamlet on Suicide," "Hamlet on Grave Diggers," "Hamlet on the Afterlife." *Hamlet* is, more than anything else, Hamlet talking on a multitude of different topics. (Melville's marginal comment on one of the soliloquies in the play: "Here is forcibly shown the great Montaigneism of Hamlet.") I find myself wanting to ditch the tired old plot altogether and just harness the voice, which is a processing machine, taking input and spitting out perspective—a lens, a distortion effect. Hamlet's very nearly final words: "Had I but the time . . . O, I could tell you." He would keep riffing forever if it weren't for the fact that the plot needs to kill him.

456

Plot isn't a tool; intelligence is. I don't derive meaning from intellect but from the illumination it pries out of unmediated experience. Though nonfiction has as much "fiction" in it as fiction does, its aims are different: the mediation between writer and reader is thinner. Serious nonfiction removes fiction's masks, stripping away monuments to civilization to arrive at truths that destroy the writer and thereby encompass the reader—the last shred of human expression before silence seizes all words. The novelist invents a story to highlight his craft. To a younger reader, stylistic bravura is a revelation of the imaginative life, but to the mature adult, craft per se isn't revelatory, merely a demonstration of cultural refinement and a parable of the power of storytelling, all in the interest of proclaiming the writer an artist. Fiction mimics interest in God's intelligent omnipotence: there's a plan (plot), no matter the story's tragedy; the most horrific story is softened by the author's presence, seeking, no matter how faintly, to educate us on the limits of disorder held together by the civilizing process of creation. Lyric essay tells a story at a baser level: irrational, plotless, characterless, or repetitiously characterized, it informs by serial enactments of the mind's processes prior to writing the story. The goal isn't to get to the point of wanting to write the story (or fulfilling society's need for it to be fictionalized); the goal is to bare the elements not as narrative but as life. Serious essay, disallowing the writer the privileged position of living only in his head, unravels within life's chaos, confirming the chaos. Fiction seeks eternal rationality. The burden shouldn't be for me to find myself in the work of the great fiction writer; he seeks to escape his head by allowing me in through exegesis, a game that pretends to reward the best chess players. I prefer essayistic impulse: violently bumping up against the other at the flashpoint of instinctual reaction. I don't want to be inside the fiction writer's head unless he first agrees to kill his characters. After two decades of playing rock 'n' roll, Lou Reed put out an album of white noise called *Metal Machine Music*—could be brilliant, could be bullshit—to get himself out of a record contract to a label he hated, but it's become influential. The advice in his liner notes: "Kill your band."

457

So: no more masters, no more masterpieces. What I want (instead of God the novelist) is self-portrait in a convex mirror.

r

autobio

458

As far as I can recall, the initial shiver of inspiration was somehow prompted by a newspaper story about an ape that, after months of coaxing by a scientist, produced the first drawing ever charcoaled by an animal; this sketch showed the bars of the poor creature's cage.

459

I wrote a story once about a man who began a very large picture, and therein was a kind of map—for example, hills, horses, streams, fishes, and woods and towers and men and all sorts of things. When the day of his death came, he found he had been making a picture of himself. That is the case with most writers.

460

In, for example, Naipaul's *A Way in the World*, Sebald's *The Emigrants*, Hilton Als's *The Women*, each chapter, when consid-

ered singly, is relatively straightforwardly biographical, but
when the book is read as a whole and tilted at just the right
angle, it refracts brilliant, harsh light back upon the author.

461

In a larger sense, all writing is autobiography: everything that
you write, including criticism and fiction, writes you as you
write it. The real question is: this massive autobiographical
writing enterprise that fills a life, this enterprise of self-
construction—does it yield only fictions? Or rather, among the
fictions of the self, the versions of the self, that it yields, are
there any that are truer than others? How do I know when I
have the truth about myself?

462

The final orbit is oneself. Who can calculate the orbit of his
own soul?

463

What personal essayists, as opposed to novelists or faux-naïf
memoirists, do: keep looking at their own lives from different
angles, keep trying to find new metaphors for the self and the
self's soul mates. The only serious journey, to me, is deeper into
self. We're all guaranteed, of course, never to fully know ourselves, which fails, somehow, to mitigate the urgency of the
journey.

464

You keep excavating yourself. You want/don't want this self-
knowledge. Tough fucking task.

465

Every documentary film, even—especially—the least self-referential, demonstrates in its every frame that an artist's chief material is himself.

466

What does it mean to write about yourself? To what degree is this a solipsistic enterprise? To what degree are we all solipsists? To what degree can solipsism gain access to the world?

467

Speaking about oneself is not necessarily offensive. A modest, truthful man speaks better about himself than about anything else, and on that subject his speech is likely to be most profitable to his hearers. If he be without taint of boastfulness, of self-sufficiency, of hungry vanity, the world will not press the charge home. It is this egotism, this perpetual reference to self, in which the charm of the essayist resides. If a man is worth knowing at all, he is worth knowing well.

468

Mad genius? Narcissistic artist? An entertainer who can't resist throwing in the kitchen sink? Viewers will make up their own definition for Nedžad Begović, the director and central character of the aptly titled *Totally Personal,* which has much to say about what it's like to live in Sarajevo, as seen through the quizzical eyes of his narrator-protagonist. Starting with his birth in 1958, Begović fills us in on what it was like to have the first TV on the block, to take loyalty oaths to Yugoslavian leader Tito and the Motherland, to get married to Amina, and to decide to make a no-budget film with a digital camera. All this and much, much more is narrated with self-deprecating humor in wonderfully accented English. The film-maker's precarious means, far from being a handicap to his storytelling, seem to inspire him to ever greater heights of imagination. He introduces whimsical theories about body parts and why the Serbian Chetniks started a war in Bosnia and what the UN forces were really doing during said war (answer: counting the number of shells fired). The film's financial and technical limitations finally converge with the serious short-ages that Bosnians experienced during the war—including no water, bread, electricity, or gasoline. Bosnians' innate creativ-ity, Begovićz seems to say, has seen them through under all cir-cumstances, just as his own imagination has created what he modestly calls his own little masterpiece. *Totally Personal.* Nedžad Begovićz. Bosnia and Herzegovina. 2004. 79 minutes. Color and B&W. In Bosnian with English subtitles. World premiere.

469
There is properly no history, only biography.

470
All that is personal soon rots; it must be packed in ice or salt.

471
I place a living cat into a steel chamber, along with a device containing a vial of hydrocyanic acid. In the chamber is a very small amount of a radioactive substance. If even a single atom of the substance decays during the test period, a relay mecha-nism will trip a hammer, which will break the vial and kill the cat. I can't know whether an atom of the substance has decayed and, consequently, can't know whether the vial has been bro-ken, the hydrocyanic acid released, and the cat killed. Since I

can't know, the cat is—according to quantum law—both dead and alive, in a superposition of states. Only when I break open the box and learn the condition of the cat is this superposition lost and the cat dead or alive. The observation or measurement itself affects the outcome; it can never be known what the outcome would have been were it not observed. . . . The writers I love tend to have Schrödinger's Paradox tattooed on their forehead: the perceiver by his very presence changes what's perceived. A work without some element of self-reflexivity feels to me falsely monumental. Without this gesture, this self-scrutiny, I don't see how anyone can even pretend to be thinking.

472

The highest as the lowest form of criticism is a mode of autobiography.

473

In *On Moral Fiction,* John Gardner explains that "the morality of art is far less a matter of doctrine than of process." He's careful to distinguish between didactic art, which teaches by "authority and force," and moral art, which "explores, open-mindedly, to learn what it should teach. The artist who begins with a doctrine to promulgate, instead of a rabble multitude of ideas and emotions, is beaten before he starts." He cautions that "the subversion of art to the purposes of propaganda leads inevitably to one or the other of the two common mistakes in bad art: overemphasis of texture, on the one hand, and manipulative structure, on the other." In *Vlemk the Box-Painter,* Gardner's first novel following his critical call to arms, he doesn't overemphasize texture—the fablelike quality of the book makes for a very simple prose—but he does manipulate structure. *Vlemk the Box-Painter* is an illustration of a thesis, a step-by-step argument for the aesthetic program presented in *On Moral Fiction.* Gardner clearly conceived *Vlemk* as the dramatization of a doctrine. He didn't discover his material in the process of creation; he began with a theory. *Vlemk* is a didactic rather than moral work of art, and Gardner's aesthetic would appear to be suspect if it can't accommodate his own fiction. . . . This review is the first thing I ever published. Its line of argument still seems to me essentially correct—John Gardner's philosophy of fiction is impossibly programmatic—but that seems pretty obvious, and all I care about now is its secret subtext: on the surface a quite standard book review, it was really my attempt to put as much ground as I could between myself and my parents' engagé moralism. Growing up in a Bay Area suburb in the 1960s and '70s, I was instructed by my mother and father to write denunciatory editorials about the (only very mildly) dictatorial high school principal; I was dragged into the city for antiwar marches what seems in memory every third weekend. In *Against Interpretation,* Susan Sontag says that the two primary, opposing artistic stances of the twentieth century are—were—Jewish moralism and homosexual aestheticism. I see my first published piece as a desperate effort to free myself from Jewish moralism; the effort shows. In college, my (Jewish) creative-writing teacher—David Milch, who went on to cowrite and coproduce the television shows *Hill Street Blues, NYPD Blue,* and *Deadwood*—told me my work suffered from the malaise of my (his) "race": a preoccupation with "narrowly moral" rather than "universally human" concerns. I was, as he hoped I'd be, near suicidal for the remainder of the term.

474

Writing enters into us when it gives us information about ourselves we're in need of at the time we're reading.

475

For Coetzee, all criticism, including his own, is autobiographical.

476

Every man's work—whether it be literature or music or pictures or architecture or anything else—is always a portrait of himself.

477

Every sound we make is a bit of autobiography.

S

persona

478

And I shall essay to be.

479

The book is written in the first person, but that *I* is the most deceptive, tricky pronoun. There are two of us. I'm a chronicler of this character at the center who is, but in a necessary sense is not, me. He doesn't have my retrospect or my leisure. He doesn't know what's around the next bend. He's ignorant of consequences. He moves through the book in a state of innocence about the future, whereas of course I as the writer, from the time I begin writing the first paragraph, do know what the future holds. I know how the story is going to turn out.

480

Painting myself for others, I have painted my inward self with colors clearer than my original ones. I have no more made my book than my book has made me.

481

Cinéma vérité looks for performers in everyday life; without them, you really haven't got footage. Some people have whatever quality it is that makes them interesting on film—a kind of self-confidence or self-assuredness mixed, perhaps, with a degree of vulnerability—and other people don't have it, but as a filmmaker you know it when you see it. You have to sense that there's something real behind the so-called performance.

482

Johnny Carson, asked to describe the difference between himself and Robert Redford, said, "I'm playing me."

483

In *Essays of Elia,* Charles Lamb turned the reader's attention to the persona, the unreliable mask of the "I," not as an immutable fact of literature but as a tool of the essayist in particular, who, if he or she wants to get personal, must first choose what to conceal. These peculiarities—the theatrical reticence, the archaism, the nostalgia, the celebration of oddity for its own sake—are regular features of Lamb's essays, and they helped to change the English (and American) idea of what an essay should be. Even when personal essayists don't flaunt their power to mislead us, even when we no longer expect belle-lettrists to write old-fashioned prose, we still expect essays to deliver that same Elian tension between the personal and the truly private and to tell stories that are digressive and inconclusive. Most of all, we expect personal essayists to speak to us from behind a stylized version of themselves, rather than give us the whole man—as Montaigne or Lamb's favorite devotional writers seem to do—or a more or less representative man like the *Spectator* of Addison and Steele. Lamb wasn't the only Romantic essayist who wrote this way. Hazlitt soon followed suit, and so did De Quincey and Hunt, but Lamb was the first. Ever since Elia, eccentricity has been the rule.

484

Autobiography can be naïvely understood as pure self-revelation or more cannily recognized as cleverly wrought subterfuge.

485

When I state myself, as the Representative of the Verse—it does not mean—me—but a supposed person.

486

I'm not interested in myself per se. I'm interested in myself as theme carrier, as host.

487

A novelist friend, who can't not write fiction but is flummoxed whenever he tries to write nonfiction directly about his own experience, read something I wrote and said he was impressed (alarmed?) by my willingness to say nearly anything about myself: "It's all about you and yet somehow it's not about you at all. How can that be?"

488

One is not important, except insofar as one's example can serve to elucidate a more widespread human trait and make readers feel a little less lonely and freakish.

489

"It must go further still: that soul must become its own betrayer, its own deliverer, the one activity, the mirror turn lamp"—which could and should serve as epigraph to Alphonse Daudet's *In the Land of Pain,* Pessoa's *The Book of Disquiet,* Michel Leiris's *Manhood: A Journey from Childhood into the Fierce Order of Virility,* Joe Brainard's *I Remember,* Grégoire Bouillier's *The Mystery Guest.*

490

Andy Kaufman went way beyond blurring the distinction between performer and persona, past the point where you wondered what separated the actor from the character; you wondered if he himself knew anymore where the boundaries were drawn. What did he get out of such performances? The joy of not telling the audience how to react, giving that decision—or maybe just the illusion of such decision making—back to the audience. Afterward, he typically stayed in character when among fellow performers, who resented being treated like civilians. On his ABC special, the vertical hold kept rolling, which the network hated because it didn't want viewers to think there was anything wrong with their TV sets when in fact the problem was by design.

491

In Lorrie Moore's story "People Like That Are the Only People Here," the putatively fictional account of a writer whose toddler is diagnosed with cancer, characters are named only by the roles they play: Mother, Husband, Baby, Surgeon, Radiologist, Oncologist. The Mother discusses the possibility—the Husband emphasizes the financial necessity—of writing about the experience. When the story was published as fiction in the *New*

Yorker, it was accompanied by a photo of Moore and a caption: "No, I can't. Not this! I write fiction. This isn't fiction." About the story, Moore has said, "It's fiction. Things didn't happen exactly that way; I reimagined everything. And that's what fiction does. Fiction can come from real-life events and still be fiction." The Mother is a writer and teacher who is already writing each scene as she experiences it. If this isn't a story about Moore and her baby, what is it about? The deep ambivalence writers have about using their personal lives to make a living. Even as the Mother agonizes about taking notes, she's diligently observing the environment, gathering data about cancer that will both help her child and (bonus!) make the story she'll write a better one. God, embodied as the manager of Marshall Field's, informs the Mother that "to know the narrative in advance is to turn yourself into a machine. What makes humans human is precisely that they do not know the future." The writer, of course, writing the story, does know what the ending will be, has planned it, lived through it. And the Mother also knows the future. Leaving the hospital with the baby, the Husband expresses gratitude for the people they've met, and the Mother responds, "For as long as I live, I never want to see any of these people again." Actually, the Mother will see these people, over and over again: she'll spend a great deal of time and effort re-creating them; writing the story, she ensures that these people will always be with her. The last two lines of the story are "These are the notes. Now, where is the money?" If the Mother is angry at the world for paying to read such a story, she's also angry at herself for profiting not only from her own life and pain but from that of her family and all the families who shared their time in the pediatric oncology ward with her. She's angry that she can't leave these people behind, or the worry behind, or the fundamental truth that a part of living, of breathing, of surviving, is to exploit our human relationships in order to live.

492

The source of my crush on Sarah Silverman? Her willingness to say unsettling things about herself, position herself as a fuck-me/fuck-you figure, a bad-good girl, a JAP who takes her JAPiness and pushes it until it becomes the culture's grotesquerie: "I was raped by a doctor—which is, you know, so bittersweet for a Jewish girl." "I don't care if you think I'm racist; I only care if you think I'm thin." "Obviously, I'm not trying to belittle the events of September eleventh; they were devastating, they were beyond devastating, and I don't want to say especially for these people or especially for these people, but especially for me, because it happened to be the same exact day that I found out that the soy chai latte was, like, 900 calories."

493

A Hero of Our Time, gentlemen, is in fact a portrait, but not of an individual; it is the aggregate of the vices of our whole generation in their fullest expression.

494

The man who writes about himself and his time is the man who writes about all people and all time.

495

Was Keats a confessional poet? When he talks about youth that grows "pale and specter-thin, and dies," he's talking about his kid brother Tom, who died of tuberculosis. But he's talking about more than that. The word *confessional* implies the need to purge oneself and to receive forgiveness for one's life. I don't think that's what confessional poetry is about at all. I think it's a poetry that comes out of the stuff of the poet's personal life, but he's trying to render this experience in more general and inclusive, or what used to be called *universal,* terms. He's presenting himself as a representative human being. He's saying, "This is what happens to us as human beings in this flawed and difficult world, where joy is rare." Sylvia Plath is certainly one of the outstanding "confessional" poets, but when Plath entitles a poem "Lady Lazarus," she's trying to connect herself to the whole tradition of pain and death and resurrection. She's not presenting herself as Sylvia Plath but as part of a larger pattern.

496

This is the wager, isn't it? It's by remaining faithful to the contingencies and peculiarities of your own experience and the vagaries of your own nature that you stand the greatest chance of conveying something universal.

497

Self-study of any seriousness aspires to myth. Thus do we endlessly inscribe and magnify ourselves.

498

A man's life of any worth is a continual allegory.

499

What is true for you in your private heart is true for all men.

500

All our stories are the same.

501

Every man has within himself the entire human condition.

502

Deep down, you know you're him.

t

ds

503

When I was seventeen, I wanted a life consecrated to art. I imagined a wholly committed art-life: every gesture would be an aesthetic expression or response. That got old fast because, unfortunately, life is filled with allergies, credit-card bills, tedious commutes, etc. Life is, in large part, rubbish. The beauty of reality-based art—art underwritten by reality hunger—is that it's perfectly situated between life itself and (unattainable) "life as art." Everything in life, turned sideways, can look like—can be—art. Art suddenly looks and is more interesting, and life, astonishingly enough, starts to be livable.

504

I was nineteen years old and a virgin, and at first I read Rebecca's journal because I needed to know what to do next and what she liked to hear. Every little gesture, every minor movement I made she passionately described and wholeheart-edly admired. When we were kissing or swimming or walking down the street, I could hardly wait to rush back to her room to find out what phrase or what twist of my body had been lauded in her journal. I loved her impatient handwriting, her purple ink, the melodrama of the whole thing. It was such a surprising and addictive respite, seeing every aspect of my being celebrated by someone else rather than excoriated by myself. She wrote, "I've never truly loved anyone the way I love D. and it's never been so total and complete, yet so unpossessing and pure, and sometimes I want to drink him in like golden water." *You* try to concentrate on your Milton midterm after reading that about yourself. . . . Weeks passed; guilt grew. I told Rebecca that I'd read her journal. Why couldn't I just live with the knowledge and let the shame dissipate over time? What was—what is—the matter with me? Do I just have a bigger self-destruct button, and like to push it harder and more incessantly, than everyone else? True, but also the language of the events was at least as erotic to me as the events themselves, and when I was no longer reading her words, I was no longer very adamantly in love with Rebecca. This is what is known as a tragic flaw.

505

Standard operating procedure for fiction writers is to disavow any but the most insignificant link between the life lived and the novel written; similarly, for nonfiction writers, the main impulse is to insist upon the unassailable verisimilitude of the book they've produced. I've written three books of fiction and twice as many books of nonfiction, and whenever I'm discussing the supposed reality of a work of nonfiction I've written, I inevitably (and rapidly) move the conversation over to a contemplation of the ways in which I've fudged facts, exaggerated my emotions, cast myself as a symbolic figure, and invented freely. So, too, whenever anyone asks me about the origins of a work of fiction, I always forget to say, *I made it all up* and instead start talking about, for lack of a better term, real life. Why can't I get my stories straight? Why do I so resist generic boundaries, and why am I so drawn to generic fissures? Why do I always seem to want to fold one form into another?

506

Both of my parents were journalists. For many years my mother was the West Coast correspondent for the *Nation*. My father wrote for dozens of left-wing publications and organizations and, until he turned ninety, was a sports reporter for a weekly newspaper in suburban San Francisco. When I was growing up, the *New York Times* was airmailed to our house every day. Mornings, I would frequently find on the kitchen counter an article neatly scissored out of the *Times* for me to read as a model of journalistic something or other. (I may have made this detail up, but it sounds right, it feels right, maybe it happened once; I'm going to leave it in.) I was the editor of my junior high school newspaper. I was the editor of my high school newspaper. Woodward and Bernstein were my heroes. My parents' heroes, interestingly enough, weren't journalists but what they called "real writers": Thomas Wolfe, John Steinbeck, Saul Bellow. My father stammered slightly, and in the verbal hothouse that was our family (dinner-table conversations always felt like a newsroom at deadline), I took his halting speech and turned it into a full-blown stutter, which not only qualified any ambition I might have had to become a journalist—I couldn't imagine how I'd ever be able to imitate my mother's acquaintance Daniel Schorr and confidently ask a question at a presidential press conference—but also made me, in general, wary of any too direct discourse. In graduate school, when I studied deconstruction, it all seemed very self-evident.

Language as self-canceling reverb that is always communicating only itself? I knew this from the inside out since I was six years old. In a stutterer's mouth and mind, everything is up for grabs. Stuttering reminds me that lyricism turned counterclockwise is a bad block; my father reminds me that Walt Whitman once said, "The true poem is the daily paper." Not, though, the daily paper as it's published: both straight-ahead journalism and airtight art are, to me, insufficient; I want instead something teetering excitedly in between.

507

I have a very vivid memory of being assigned to read *The Grapes of Wrath* as a junior in high school and playing hooky from my homework to read *Fear and Loathing: On the Campaign Trail '72*. Steinbeck's humorlessness, sentimentality, and sledgehammer symbolism hardly had a chance against Hunter Thompson's comedy, nihilism, and free association. I loved how easily *Fear and Loathing* mixed reportage, or pseudo-reportage, with glimmers of autobiography. My sister and I had a rather fierce debate about the authenticity of a scene in which Thompson has a conversation with Richard Nixon at an adjoining urinal. She wrote to Thompson to ask which of us was right. I was wrong (if memory, that inveterate trickster, is accurate, he called me a "pencil-necked geek"), but still it was liberating to read a work open-ended enough that the thought could occur to you that some of this stuff had to be made up or, even better, you couldn't quite tell.

508

During freshman orientation, I joined the *Brown Daily Herald,* but by February I'd quit—actually, I was fired—when there was a big brouhaha surrounding the fact that I'd made stuff up. I started spending long hours in the Marxist bookstore just off campus, reading and eating my lunch bought at McDonald's; I loved slurping coffee milkshakes while reading and rereading Sartre's *The Words*. I closed the library nearly every night for four years; at the end of one particularly productive work session, I actually scratched into the concrete wall above my carrel, "I shall dethrone Shakespeare." (Since I was a teenager, I've been going to the Oregon Shakespeare Festival, which mixes Shakespearean and non-Shakespearean plays. I recently saw the understudy—with twenty-four hours' notice—play the lead in *Cyrano de Bergerac*. Every fifteen minutes or so, he'd call out to the assistant director, sitting in the front row, to provide the line for him. This Cyrano's crippled eloquence, the actor's grace, his refusal to wilt, was much more moving to me than anything in the play or any other play.)

509

As a sophomore at Brown, in 1976, I was trying to figure out how I wanted to write. One of my teachers was John Hawkes, who wrote, "Beyond the edge of town, past tar-covered poor houses and a low hill bare except for fallen electric poles, was the institution and it sent its delicate and isolated buildings trembling over the gravel and cinder floor of the valley." Hawkes was an inspiring teacher, but I had no instinct for the symbolist surrealism of which he was a master; his work offered no guideposts for me. My other writing teacher in college was R. V. Cassill, who wrote, "Cory Johnson was shelling corn in the crib on his farm. He had a rattletrap old sheller that he was rather proud of. Some of its parts—the gears and the rust-pitted flywheel bored for a hand crank—had come from a machine in use on this farm for longer than Cory had lived." I wasn't connected to place in the way Cassill was—I knew virtually nothing and didn't care to know about the San Francisco suburb in which I grew up—and though he also was an exceptionally fine teacher, his work (beautifully crafted as it was) didn't trigger anything particularly crucial for me, either.

510

My college girlfriend and I shared a summer house in the Catskills. We'd go to the general store and have a slightly off-kilter conversation with someone about, say, a lawn mower, then in the middle of the night she'd wake me up and ask if I wanted to read, say, a fourteen-page fantasia entitled "Monologue of the Lawn Mower." This happened over and over again that summer, so much so that I came to dread doing anything very dramatic with her, lest she knock me over with her magnum opus.

511

On my breakneck tour of European capitals the summer after graduation, I carried in my backpack two books: *One Hundred Years of Solitude* and *Swann's Way.* Just as Steinbeck's allegory had bored me and Thompson's meditation on the real had enthralled me, García Márquez failed to hold my attention and Proust became a years-long addiction. I loved how Marcel was both sort of the author and sort of a character; how the book was both a work of fiction and a philosophical treatise; how it could talk about whatever it wanted to for as long as it wanted to; how its deepest plot was uncovering the process by which it came into being.

512

In graduate school, where my first fictional instructor said she wished she were as famous to the world as she was to herself, and my second fictional instructor said that if he had to do it over again, he'd have become a screenwriter, I was surrounded by older and better writers who wrote more relaxedly, whereas I was trying to sound like Thomas Hardy. *Oh, I see,* I remember realizing, *you write out of your own experience. You write in your own voice and don't try to write literature per se.* I don't know why I needed to learn this, but I did. *And if part of your childhood was spent watching* Get Smart, *it's okay to mention that; don't pretend you grew up in France.* This was hugely revelatory, though it seems self-evident now.

513

Perhaps under the influence of the Iowa Writers' Workshop, which when I was there in the late 1970s was a citadel of tradi-tionalism (as, for that matter, it still is), my first novel couldn't have fit any more snugly inside the rubric of linear realistic novel and is the only book I've written that is pretty much whole-cloth invention. But I wanted to write a book whose loyalty wasn't just to art but to life—my life. I wanted to be part of the process, part of the problem.

514

For quite a while I wrote in a fairly traditional manner—two linear, realistic novels and dozens of conventionally plotted stories. I'm not a big believer in major epiphanies, especially those that occur in the shower, but I had one nearly twenty years ago, and it occurred in the shower: I had the sudden intu-ition that I could take various fragments of things—aborted stories, outtakes from novels, journal entries, lit crit—and build a story out of them. I really had no idea what the story would be about; I just knew I needed to see what it would look like to set certain shards in juxtaposition to other shards. Now I have trouble working any other way, but I can't emphasize enough how strange it felt at the time, working in this modal mode. The initial hurdle (and much the most important one) was being willing to follow this inchoate intuition, yield to the prompting, not fight it off, not retreat to SOP. I thought the story probably had something to do with obsession; I wonder where I got that idea—rummaging through boxes of old papers, riffling through drawers and computer files, crawling around on my hands and knees on the living room floor, looking for bits and pieces I thought might cohere. Scissoring and taping together paragraphs from previous projects, moving them around in endless combinations, completely rewriting some sections, jettisoning others, I found a clipped, hard-bitten tone entering the pieces. My work had never been sweet, but this seemed harsher, sharper, even a little hysterical. That tone is, in a sense, the plot of the story. I thought I was writing a story about obsession. I was really writing a story about the hell of obsessive ego. It was exciting to see how part of something I had originally written as an exegesis of Joyce's "The Dead" could now be turned sideways and used as the final, bruising insight into someone's psyche. All literary possibilities opened up for me with this story. The way my mind thinks—everything is connected to everything else—suddenly seemed transportable into my writing. I could play all the roles I want to play (reporter, fantasist, autobiographer, essayist, critic). I could call on my writerly strengths, bury my writerly weaknesses, be as smart on the page as I wanted to be. I'd found a way to write that seemed true to how I am in the world.

515

Conversion narrative the second: in the mid-1990s, I thought I was working on my fourth novel, but the novel collapsed—I simply could not commit the requisite resources to character and scene and plot—and out of that emerged my first work of "nonfiction," *Remote.* What sent me like Alice down the rabbit hole, never to emerge again on terra firma, were Renata Adler's *Speedboat,* George W. S. Trow's *Within the Context of No Context,* Ross McElwee's *Sherman's March* (shortly after I'd watched it, someone said to me that it was "the first film I've ever seen in which I recognized the South in which I lived"; I misheard her as saying "the *self* in which I lived"), Spalding Gray's *Swimming to Cambodia,* Sandra Bernhard's *Without You I'm Nothing,* Denis Leary's *No Cure for Cancer,* Rick Reynolds's *Only the Truth Is Funny,* Chris Rock's *Bring the Pain,* Art Spiegelman's *Maus,* Anne Carson's "Essay on the Difference between Men and Women." What is it about these works I liked and like so much? The confusion between field report and self-portrait; the confusion between fiction and nonfiction; the author-narrators' use of themselves, as personae, as representatives of feeling states; the antilinearity; the simultaneous bypassing and stalking of artifice-making machinery; the absolute seriousness, phrased as comedy; the violent torque of their beautifully idiosyncratic voices.

516

Dear William,

I admire your work and was a big fan of your lecture, so the misunderstanding between us is particularly painful to me. I take these issues very seriously and am, I think, alert to nuances in this regard, as I hope my work demonstrates. Here's my view of what happened: you mentioned your student's interest in reading novels that deal in different ways with a narrator's willingness or unwillingness to discuss incest or abuse. I thought of Kathryn Harrison's *The Kiss,*

which I didn't expect to like but which, to my surprise, I did.
If you dislike the book, I'd be curious to know why, since
I respect your literary acumen as it was revealed in your
lecture. When I suggested *The Kiss,* you—rather cavalierly,
I thought—dismissed it as beneath consideration. You said
something like, "On principle, I'd never have one of my
students read *that.*" To me, the implication was that you
didn't like "memoir" or that you didn't like books that had
gotten too much attention or that you'd read some of the
withering reviews and had perhaps prejudged it (as I had). So
I was genuinely asking you, "Have you read it?" My tone was
probably a little querulous, for which I apologize, but that
had nothing to do with the fact that you're African American
and everything to do with my frustration at times with the
extremely traditional aesthetic that predominates at this
conference. I find that the kind of work to which I'm most
drawn is often condescended to here, and my snappishness
had to do with that. When Melanie said, "You can't assign
The Kiss; it's memoir," I practically shouted at her, "Writing
is writing. Every act of composition is a work of fiction"—an
argument I'm going to try to make or at least explore in my
lecture on Thursday. Let's continue the conversation. Write
me back, or let's get together to talk.

Best,
David

517

I'm hopelessly, futilely drawn toward representations of the
real, knowing full well how invented such representations are.
I'm bored by out-and-out fabrication, by myself and others;
bored by invented plots and invented characters. I want to

explore my own damn, doomed character. I want to cut to the absolute bone. Everything else seems like so much gimmickry.

518

For me, anyway, the fictional construct rarely takes you deeper into the material that you want to explore. Instead, it takes you deeper into the fictional construct, into the technology of narrative, of plot, of place, of scene, of characters. In most novels I read, the narrative completely overwhelms whatever it was the writer supposedly set out to explore in the first place.

519

I have a strong reality gene. I don't have a huge pyrotechnic imagination that luxuriates in other worlds. People say, "It was so fascinating to read this novel that took place in Iceland. I just loved living inside another world for two weeks." That doesn't, I must say, interest me that much.

520

The center of the artistic process—for me—is the attempt to transform a particular feeling, insight, sorrow into a metaphor and then make that metaphor ramify so it holds everything, everything in the world.

521

The only way I've found I can live, literarily, is by carving out my own space between the interstices of fiction and non-.

522

I'm constantly scribbling mini-epiphanies in my notebook, but I make sure my handwriting is illegible enough that half an hour later I can't quite decipher the crucial revelation.

523

The 2009 Pulitzer Prize for Fiction was awarded to Elizabeth Strout for *Olive Kitteredge*. Have I read it? No. Will I? No. I come not to bury Strout (or Kitteredge) but to dispraise fiction, which has never seemed less central to the culture's sense of itself. I'm drawn, instead, to "confession" because I like the way the temperature in the room goes up when I say, "I did this" (even if I really didn't). I like a documentary frame around the material for the way it promises news of the world, even though I couldn't care less what happened and what didn't, and I know there's no way to mark the difference, since memory is a dream machine, a de facto fiction-making operation. I can't write a note to my daughter's eleventh-grade humanities teacher (Hi, Suzanne!) without little lies leaking in. Whatever can be said gets said. Language is a weird, somewhat whimsical governor. When I read fiction, I look for what's real, try to identify the source models. When I read nonfiction, I look for problems with the facts. I recognize no difference along the truth continuum between my very autobiographical novels and my frequently fib-filled books of nonfiction. Or is this the ultimate fiction, the autobiographer slipping the bonds of actuality now that his adventures have gone public?

u

alone

524

Democracy turns man's imagination away from externals to concentrate on himself alone. Democratic peoples may amuse themselves momentarily by looking at nature, but it is about themselves that they are really excited. Here, and here alone, are the true springs of poetry among them, and those poets, I believe, who do not draw inspiration from these springs will lose their hold over the audience they intend to charm.

525

Not only does democracy make every man forget his ancestors, but it hides his descendants and separates his contemporaries from him; it throws him back forever upon himself alone and threatens in the end to confine him entirely within the solitude of his own heart.

526

For ten years I traveled all over Hungary, visiting the homeless and the poor. I interviewed gypsies living in dire conditions and Hungarian workers, many of whom came from peasant backgrounds. In all, I did some two thousand interviews. The more people I met, the more life stories I heard and the more persuaded I became that it is almost impossible to know someone else completely. We radiate feelings to others, but ultimately we are alone. For me, the essence of life is how we handle our loneliness.

527

While there is no objective world beyond our individual capacity to comprehend it—that is, nothing outside of ourselves to let us off the hook for our personal failures—the individual must still deny this subjectivity in order to be, to exist, to effect his particular project. He must lose himself in order to find himself.

528

We are always only in our own company.

529

We are adrift, alone in the cosmos, wreaking monstrous violence on one another out of frustration and pain.

530

Personal lyricism is the outcry of prisoner to prisoner from the cell in solitary where each is confined for the duration of his life.

531

Nothing can make of Kafka a bad writer, but there were things that lay outside his ken: the communal, the shared, the necessary social lie, and, most significantly, other people. That Kafka finally comprehended this lack in himself, that he measured the shape and depth of his own wound—this is what makes him an information bureau of the human condition.

532

In the end one experiences only oneself.

533

All alone is all we are.

534

If we were not all so interested in ourselves, life would be so uninteresting that none of us would be able to endure it.

535

I do not know if it has ever been noted before that one of the main characteristics of life is discreteness. Unless a film of flesh envelops us, we die. Man exists only insofar as he is separated from his surroundings. The cranium is a space traveler's helmet. Stay inside or you perish. Death is divestment; death is communion. It may be wonderful to mix with the landscape, but to do so is the end of the tender ego.

536

The difference between you and me is that I die alone.

537

We are and we are not.

V

it is
much more
important
to be
oneself than
anything else

538

I find myself saying briefly and prosaically that it is much more important to be oneself than anything else.

539

Listen carefully to first criticisms of your work. Note carefully just what it is about your work that the critics don't like—then cultivate it. That's the part of your work that's individual and worth keeping.

540

Anything you do will be an abuse of somebody else's aesthetics.

541

What you respond to in any work of art is the artist's struggle against his or her own limitations.

542

Write yourself naked, from exile, and in blood.

543

Of all that might be omitted in thinking, the worst is to omit your own being.

544

This isn't just an epigram—life is more successfully looked at from a single window, after all.

545

First person is where you can be more interesting; you don't have to be much but a stumbling fool. And I find this often leads to the more delightful expedition. The wisdom there is more precious than in the sage overview, which in many writers makes me nearly puke.

546

When it is suggested that acting can also fuel neurosis and self-involvement, Ms. Leigh suddenly exudes the polish and intensity she displays on the screen. She's decided, for a moment, to perform. "Well," she says with a toss of her head and a wave of her hand, "of course, but who isn't self-involved?"

547

Contemporary culture makes pilgrimage impossible. Experience is always secondhand, planned and described for one's consumption by others in advance. Even the rare, authentically direct experience is spoiled by self-consciousness. We're doomed to an imitation of life.

548

I took Tomaž Šalamun to see the Hans Hoffmann show at the Berkeley museum. We walked through Hoffmann trying on everybody's form of abstract expressionism, the de Kooning–like paintings, the Newman-like paintings, the Gottlieb-like paintings, and the Pollock and the Rothko types, all of them done with great boldness and vigor. We came back out into the sunlight, and Tomaž said, "Poor man, he had no fate."

risk

549

It is not instruction but provocation that I can receive from another soul.

550

Lionel Trilling, unwilling to pay the cost of exposing himself to ridicule, envied the sacrifice—in Hemingway—of all the usual grounds of personal pride and self-respect.

551

I thought of myself as an imperfect writer who needed to perfect himself, perfect his language and style, and all of a sudden that was a suffocating project that I had to break with.

552

It is indeed becoming more and more difficult, even senseless, for me to write an official English. And more and more my own language appears to me like a veil that must be torn apart in order to get at the things, or the Nothingness, behind it. Grammar and Style—to me they seem to have become as irrelevant as a Victorian bathing suit or the imperturbability of a true gentleman. A mask. Let us hope the time will come when language is most efficiently used where it is being most efficiently misused. As we cannot eliminate language all at once, we should at least leave nothing undone that might contribute to its falling into disrepute. To bore one hole after another in it, until what lurks behind it (be it something or nothing) begins to seep through: I cannot imagine a higher goal for a writer today.

553
Literary intensity is inseparable from self-indulgence and self-exposure.

554
You want to put in a little bit of David—the safe part of David—the David that you wouldn't be afraid to show anybody, but there is a David that you don't want to be in the film, and that's what you should try to put in, if you don't dare face yourself other ways. Confess things to the camera. Say the things you're most ashamed of, things you don't want to remember, things you don't want anybody to know. Maybe that way there'll be some truth.

555
If your picture isn't any good, you're not standing close enough.

556
Purity of heart is to will one thing.

557

I know of nothing more difficult than knowing who you are and having the courage to share the reasons for the catastrophe of your character with the world.

558

—the sense that the author is writing for her very life.

559

If you listen, I'll save your life. If you don't listen, I'll die. Also, if you don't listen, you'll die a lot harder. There's the exchange.

560

Let a man go to the bottom of what he is and believe in that.

561

Why should we honor only those that die upon the field of battle? A man may show as reckless a courage in entering into the abyss of himself.

562

The way to write is to throw your body at the mark when all your arrows are spent.

563

There he stood, suffering embarrassment for the mistake of thinking that one may pluck a single leaf from the laurel tree of art without paying for it with his life.

564

The spectacle of baring the naked soul is meant to awaken the sympathy of the reader, who is apt to forgive the essayist's self-absorption in return for the warmth of his or her candor.

565

Vulnerability doesn't mean that anything personal goes. The exposure of the self who is also a spectator has to take us somewhere we would otherwise not get to. It has to be essential to the argument, not a decorative flourish, not exposure for its own sake. Efforts at self-revelation fail not because the personal voice has been used, but because it has been poorly used, leaving unscrutinized the connection, intellectual and emotional, between the observer and the observed.

566

We have too many things and not enough forms.

567

For if there is still one hellish, truly accursed thing in our time, it is our artistic dallying with forms, instead of being like victims burnt at the stake, signaling through the flames.

568

Watching Dave Chapelle a few years ago at the height of his fame and anxiety, I was in constant fear/excitement that he was going to go completely out of control and be taken off the stage in a straitjacket.

569

I might look like Robert Ford, but I feel just like a Jesse James.

570

Whaddya rebelling against?
  Whaddya got?

571

Who is it that can tell me who I am?

572

If you are alone, you are wholly your own.

573

To write only according to the rules laid down by masterpieces signifies that one is not a master but a pupil.

574

He who follows another will never overtake him.

575

You can always recognize the pioneers by the number of arrows in their back.

576

I think "circling the wagons" and "defending the fortress" metaphors are a little misplaced. The barbarians at the gate are usually willing to negotiate a little, and the guys in the fort usually end up yelling, "We're the only good thing in the world and you guys don't understand it," at which point the barbarians shrug, knock down your walls with amazingly powerful weapons, and put a parking lot over your sacred grounds. If they're in a really good mood, they put up a pyramid of skulls.

577

I've never heard of a crime that I could not imagine committing myself.

X

let me
tell you
what your
book is
about

578

Big surprise: I love the book, love it to death. Which is what
the book's about—loving art to death/loving it against death. I
thought the individual essays would intertwine, but I had no
idea (neither did you, probably) how beautifully and powerfully they would build. At some point, maybe halfway through, I
thought, Jonathan has to say, *I'm the disappointment artist*—how
can he say this and not have it seem heavy-handed? But there it
is, in the last essay, and it just explodes the book, forcing the
reader to retrospectively redefine what he's been reading all
along: as bildungsroman, as often indirect confession, as serious though also very funny cri de coeur. In the individual
essays, and in the book as a whole, the pattern recurs over and
over: a self declares itself; a text emerges as countertext to the
self; the text becomes heroic or the generator of the text
becomes a heroic figure, a parental figure, an authority figure
of some kind; gaps emerge; the text can't get talked about
directly; what gets talked about is the culture surrounding the

narrator, the culture surrounding the text; we keep circling self, circling text, keep searching, can't quite access self, can't quite access text, but we can access the space between the text and the self. That space is magical. That space is oddly redemptive. In that space Lethem will live.

579

Rusty's problem is that he takes things too literally. He's too much the romantic, too much the lover, too sweet, too full of feeling, too precise. On the other hand, this is all just rationalization for why he's fat and drunk and alone. And I love the way these two visions compete against each other. The book is a beautiful defense of the "unlived" life, life lived in a childlike state, in obeisance to the ideals of youth. He wants to be flawless in a flawed world; it ain't gonna happen. I found it enormously moving, especially at the end, when Rusty takes off his hairpiece and just stands naked, as it were, in front of his own life, in front of his own mortality. Confronting the abyssal within himself, he meditates upon his own isolation, his separation from love, his scary courtship of death, or at least a solitude unto death.

580

My view of the book is that, staging itself as an anthropology of the 1960s, it's mainly interested in using that theater as a way to get at the endless American dilemma—dream of self v. dream of community. Emerson v. Thoreau. Freud v. Marx. (Freud and Emerson win in a landslide.) Which couldn't be more germane to the current horror show—fanaticism in the putative service of justice. Virtually every character is locked into his or her own, somewhat rigid definition of the just and true, but the book isn't; the book is as nimble-footed as it could possibly be, and so page by page it's showing us the way to nothing less than intellectual and psychic and emotional freedom (not happiness, but freedom). You're brave in your willingness to believe—let your characters believe—in a variety of religions and then patiently dismantle each of these hope havens (nevertheless acknowledging their necessity). The ending is perfect, in that way—illusions overthrown, but somehow the living live on.

581

There's no higher praise in my lexicon than to call something an essay, an *essai,* an attempt at understanding, and each of the ~74 sections reads as a dramatized essay about illusion (subset America). There are different kinds of fiction by which people maintain order—marriage, drink, law, money, the web—and what the book does is pit Tom (Sawyer?), (Huck?) Finn, and Chick against this civilizing order. They know that each world one invents is an illusion, whereas the people on the opposite side of the waxwings think the illusion they're inhabiting is somehow "reality." I'm making the book sound more allegorical than it is, but it constantly rhymes stranger/danger with land of illusion; that's its braiding action: American society encourages (requires?) each person to specialize in the insane rhetoric of niche marketing, which that person then thinks is the world. This is the opening book in one trilogy, but it also closes another trilogy, and I see this book in close relation to *Bad Land* and *Passage to Juneau.* In *Bad Land,* they and you discover that paradise is dust. In *Passage,* you study chaos theory, only to realize your life has its own riptides. In *Waxwings,* all life on land seems to be a constant whirlpool, an illusion-making machine, and the characters the book sympathizes with know this, revel in this.

582

All season long, the Red Sox had the rational calculation (via Bill James) of bullpen by committee, then in the eighth inning of game seven, Grady Little went with pure instinct: go with the godhead. This may seem like a bit of a stretch, and a painful one at that, but to me that's what the book is about— two different kinds of memory: rational memory and instinctive memory, and the way one (sex instinct) of necessity overrides the other. Many of the reviews emphasized how this is a delightful novel about a H'wood childhood, etc., but in my reading, you're using this memory machine only as a way to get at how every self is split (cf., for instance, how part 2 is a clear rereading of part 1), how every image can be flipped, and especially how celebrity iconography plays into that. The photo at the very beginning and the photo at the very end beautifully evoke the inhuman perfection of the house, the quite human disquiet on the boys' faces. You're relentless in what you're willing to get to about the relation between sexuality and maternity, sex and imagination, e.g., the amazing visit to whorehouse and porn film therein. All of which is to say that I think of this book as (not to put too fine or famous a point on it) your *Tempest*—your meditation on the simultaneity of creation/destruction in the remembering imagination and your extraordinarily serious grappling with the psychic sources/sores of that imagination.

583

I see the movement of the poems as a working out of the narcissist dilemma. The speaker moves from American narcissism to universal luck. The book feels so lived-in and hard-won. I love your willingness to be wrong, dumb, blind, embarrassing.

584

The target of Melanie Thernstrom's *The Dead Girl* is, I think, an interesting one: the dead girl is her friend but also, of course, herself; *Investigation into the Death of Logan* is an investigation into the death of many things, not least of which is your own psyche. One of the great passages is when we learn that your sister has two children, one brother has two children, and you and Donald don't have children. With the death of the father, the world seems to stop for these two sons, especially you. The book beautifully interweaves fiction and nonfiction, history and memoir; all the categories have gotten emptied out, as how could they not be when the authority figure of the father has been erased? Even the fact that there's relatively little of your own writing per se (and instead mainly quotation) is interesting; it's as if you can't assume author/ity role in absence of your father. I really admire your willingness to talk about the violence within yourself and within your family: it's a military family, drawn to war history and to the invention of gun-related gizmos. The book is a detective story on at least three levels: first, it's quite suspenseful as to what happened to your father (was he the victim of friendly fire or was he murdered by Vietcong or did he commit suicide?); second, the interior drama of the state of the family, especially you and how you're coping or not coping with all this information, all this knowledge; third, it's a meditation, I think, on knowledge itself. I'm making this all sound rather arty and dry, but the book has tremendous courage, great honesty, vulnerability, power. I feel like I finally got to know "you": you unveil yourself layer by layer. A while ago the imaginative thing—the supposedly great thing—would have been to write a "novel about Vietnam," but I just feel in my bones how little I could read that. Now the great thing, the courageous thing, is this—this weird memoir as history/history as memoir, this laying oneself open as an historical text, this reading of history as a wound to the self.

585

The title starts out meaning "I'm doing well," then it comes to mean "Well, I'm not sure how I'm doing," and then by the end of the book it comes to mean "I'm at the bottom of the fucking well, as is everyone." That's why "It was wonderful how cool people could be" is such a brutal last line: the book has demonstrated exactly the opposite. I think of each of the separate stories here as stanzas in one long tone poem, a lyric meditation on the doomed human animal. In the first story, "someone had been fouled," and while referring nominally to the game, it really refers to "fouling" in the sense of fouling your own body and in a more cosmic sense the feeling that there's a deep metaphysical foul that can't get made up. The book is trapped in an endless feedback loop—this is related to the addictions of sex and drugs and belief—and it has the effect of making everything feel extremely echoic: sounds and tones and themes constantly recur. You relentlessly investigate the ways in which people posit a belief in something and the way that belief crashes, self-destructively, but also because it's just the nature of things. People invest in, say, a game, a body (your own or someone else's), a drug, and this hope always turns to nothing, or at least it never delivers the drug the way you thought it would. The high changes or becomes a low or fucks you up in a way you hadn't counted on. An example of this is the wonderful moment when for once someone actually gets what he wants—scores the winning basket—but it gets called off because it's after the buzzer. It's endless, this not getting what you want.

586

I think without a doubt it's your best book—your most ambitious and synoptic. I could, I fear, write a long essay concerning the very conflicted feelings that the book engendered in me. I find that I love arguing with it and, true to my fashion, tend to question my arguments. I want to put up a quasi–chamber of commerce defense of Seattle v. your definition of it as Loserville, but I suspect that I need to believe in this simply as a way to convince myself that I'm living somewhere that has freed up rather than stunted my work. Nevertheless, I think of Seattle as the capital of conventional ambition foresworn and, in its place, a deeper, stranger, more powerful ambition substituted (q.v. that essay of yours many years ago about the BBC film crew not getting Seattle, in which you explained how Seattle presents to outsiders a façade of Sleepytown USA in order to keep the world at bay as it goes about creating successes according to its own, more idiosyncratic and exacting standards). A crucial line is about Brewster as "East-Coastern, trite." So much of East Coast groupthink is, in my experience, hopelessly truistic; what Seattle represents to me is separation from that, quirky rejection of the status quo. At its worst, this translates into people who don't have a clue; at its best, it's James Acord. As someone who grew up in California and moved here from New York, I'm probably doubly guilty of imposing my imported vision of Seattle. If Seattle is locus only of ambition abandoned, then why is nearly every chapter devoted to someone who managed to succeed, and succeed gigantically—Cobain, Gates, Bezos, Schultz, McCaw, et al.? Your book has a beautiful thesis that makes extraordinary sense of 150 years, but in so doing, doesn't it exaggerate somewhat? E.g., didn't Curt Warner just fumble? Certainly he didn't "willfully" fumble. And this is where the big break comes for me: that "willfully" is very much *your* "willfully." It really is a love story: your willed, "self-pitying" version of Seattle. It's not meant to be literal or accurate in a strictly sociological sense; it's meant to be true to what you need to be true—best read as a deeply personal document of a narrator's obsessive love for a city in private, subjective, and metaphorical terms.

587

These "Let me tell you what your book is about" encomia are all notes I wrote to friends about their books. My impulse is always to push the book toward abstraction, toward sadness, toward darkness, toward doubleness, toward seventeen types of ambiguity. I always try to read form as content, style as meaning. The book is always, in some sense, stutteringly, about its own language. I'm always framing myself and the author as the lone founts of dark wisdom; I'm always the exponent of airy despair; I never touch ground. *Metaphysical* is big. In my formulation, the subject of the book is never what it appears to be. I frequently say that the book is seen to be about X when really it's about Y. I always read the book as an allegory, as a disguised philosophical argument. *Existence* is frequently mentioned, as are *human, animal, sex, fuck,* and *violence.* I love the words *powerfully* and *enormously* and *relentlessly* and *bottomlessly.* I use *investigation* and *exploration* and *excavation* and *examination* and *rigorous* over and over. What would I do without *meditation?* There's always an implied love story between me and the writer—me loving the book, loving the writer. *Candor* is key—being willing to say what no one else is willing to say. The act of writing is inevitably viewed as an act of courage (*brave* is all over the place). Life's difficult, maybe even a drag; language is (slim) solace. No one else gets what you're doing; I alone get it. You and me, babe. *Intimacy. Urgency.* We alone get life. Let me explain your book—the *text*—to yourself. Let me tell you what your book is about. Life is shit. We are shit. This, alone, will save us—this communication.

manifesto

588

It's a commonplace that every book needs to find its own form, but how many do?

589

If you want to write serious books, you must be ready to break the forms.

590

All great works of literature either dissolve a genre or invent one. *Let Us Now Praise Famous Men. Nadja. Cane. Oh, What a Blow That Phantom Gave Me!* "The Moon in Its Flight." *Wisconsin Death Trip. Letters to Wendy's.*

591

We evaluate artists by how much they are able to rid themselves of convention.

592

Jazz as jazz—jazzy jazz—is pretty well finished. The interesting stuff is all happening on the fringes of the form where there are elements of jazz and elements of all sorts of other things as well. Jazz is a trace, but it's not a defining trace. Something similar is happening in prose. Although great novels—novelly novels—are still being written, a lot of the most interesting things are happening on the fringes of several forms.

593

Still (very still), at the heart of "literary culture" is the big, blockbuster novel by middle-of-the-road writers, the run-of-the-mill four-hundred-page page-turner. Amazingly, people continue to want to read that.

594

The Corrections, say: I couldn't read that book if my life depended on it. It might be a "good" novel or it might be a "bad" novel, but something has happened to my imagination, which can no longer yield to the earnest embrace of novelistic form.

595

Is it possible that contemporary literary prizes are a bit like the federal bailout package, subsidizing work that is no longer remotely describing reality?

596

If literary terms were about artistic merit and not the rules of convenience, about achievement and not safety, the term *realism* would be an honorary one, conferred only on work that actually builds unsentimental reality on the page, that matches the complexity of life with an equally rich arrangement in language. It would be assigned no matter the stylistic or linguistic method, no matter the form. This, alas, would exclude many writers who believe themselves to be realistic, most notably those who seem to equate writing with operating a massive karaoke machine.

597

A novel, for most readers—and critics—is primarily a "story." A true novelist is one who knows how to "tell a story." To "tell a story well" is to make what one writes resemble the schemes people are used to—in other words, their ready-made idea of reality. But a work of art, like the world, is a living form. It's in its form that its reality resides.

598

Urgency attaches itself now more to the tale taken directly from life than one fashioned by the imagination out of life.

599

I want the veil of "let's pretend" out. I don't like to be carried into purely fanciful circumstances. The never-never lands of the imagination don't interest me that much. Beckett decided that everything was false to him, almost, in art, with its designs and formulae. He wanted art, but he wanted it right from life. He didn't like, finally, that Joycean voice that was too abundant, too Irish, endlessly lyrical, endlessly allusive. He went into French to cut down. He wanted to directly address desperate individual existence, which bores many readers. I find him a joyous writer, though; his work reads like prayer. You don't have to think about literary allusions but experience itself. That's what I want from the voice. I want it to transcend artifice.

600

This is life lived on high alert.

601

Nearly all writing, up to the present, has been a search for the "beautiful illusion."

602

Nowhere do you get the feeling of a writer deforming his medium in order to say what has never been said before, which is to me the mark of great writing.

603

Very well. I am not in search of the "beautiful illusion."

604

Critics can't believe that the power to make us feel our one and only life, as very few novelists actually do these days, has come from a memoirist, a nonfiction truth-speaker who has entered our common situation and is telling the story we now want told, but it has.

605

There's inevitably something terribly contrived about the standard novel; you can always feel the wheels grinding and going on.

606

If you write a novel, you sit and weave a little narrative. If you're a romantic writer, you write novels about men and women falling in love, give a little narrative here and there, etc. And it's okay, but it's of no account. Novel qua novel is a form of nostalgia.

607

There is more to be pondered in the grain and texture of life than traditional fiction allows. The work of essayists is vital precisely because it permits and encourages self-knowledge in a way that is less indirect than fiction, more open and speculative.

608

One would like to think that the personal essay represents basic research on the self, in ways that are allied with science and philosophy.

609

The poem and the essay are more intimately related than any two genres, because they're both ways of pursuing problems, or maybe trying to solve problems—*The Dream Songs,* the long prologue to *Slaughterhouse-Five,* pretty much all of Philip Larkin and Anne Carson, Annie Dillard's *For the Time Being.* Maybe these works succeed, maybe they fail, but at least they all attempt to clarify the problem at hand. They're journeys, pursuits of knowledge. One could say that fiction, metaphorically, is a pursuit of knowledge, but ultimately it's a form of entertainment. I think that, at the very least, essays and poems more directly and more urgently attempt to figure out something about the world. Which is why I can't read novels anymore, with very few exceptions, the exceptions being those novels so meditative they're barely disguised essays. David Markson's *This Is Not a Novel, Reader's Block, Vanishing Point, The Last Novel.* Coetzee's *Elizabeth Costello.* Kundera's *Immortality.* Most of Houellebecq. Doctorow's *The Book of Daniel.* Benjamin Constant's *Adolphe.* Lydia Davis, everything.

610

The kinds of novels I like are ones which bear no trace of being novels.

611

Only the suspect artist starts from art; the true artist draws his material elsewhere: from himself. There's only one thing worse than boredom—the fear of boredom—and it's this fear I experience every time I open a novel. I have no use for the hero's life, don't attend to it, don't even believe in it. The genre, having squandered its substance, no longer has an object. The character is dying out; the plot, too. It's no accident that the only novels deserving of interest today are those in which, once the universe is disbanded, nothing happens—e.g., *Tristram Shandy, Notes from Underground,* Camus's *The Fall,* Thomas Bernhard's *Correction,* Duras's *The Lover,* Barry Hannah's *Boomerang.*

612

What the lyric essay inherits from the public essay is a fact-hungry pursuit of solutions to problems, while from the personal essay it takes a wide-eyed dallying in the heat of predicaments. Lyric essays seek answers yet seldom seem to find them. They may arise out of a public essay that never manages to prove its case, may emerge from the stalk of a personal essay to sprout out and meet "the other," may start out as travelogues that forget where they are or as prose poems that refuse quick conclusions, may originate as lines that resist being broken or full-bodied paragraphs that start slimming down. They're hybrids that perch on the fence between the willed and the felt. A lyric essay is an oxymoron: an essay that's also a lyric, a kind of logic that wants to sing, an argument that has no chance of proving out.

613

An essay that becomes a lyric is an essay that has killed itself.

614

There are no facts, only art.

615

What actually happened is only raw material; what the writer makes of what happened is all that matters.

616

Once upon a time there will be readers who won't care what imaginative writing is called and will read it for its passion, its force of intellect, and its formal originality.

617

Never again will a single story be told as though it were the only one.

z

coda

618

Part of what I enjoy in documentary is the sense of banditry. To loot someone else's life or sentences and make off with a point of view, which is called "objective" because one can make anything into an object by treating it this way, is exciting and dangerous. Let us see who controls the danger.

appendix

This book contains hundreds of quotations that go unacknowledged in the body of the text. I'm trying to regain a freedom that writers from Montaigne to Burroughs took for granted and that we have lost. Your uncertainty about whose words you've just read is not a bug but a feature.

A major focus of *Reality Hunger* is appropriation and plagiarism and what these terms mean. I can hardly treat the topic deeply without engaging in it. That would be like writing a book about lying and not being permitted to lie in it. Or writing a book about destroying capitalism but being told it can't be published because it might harm the publishing industry.

However, Random House lawyers determined that it was necessary for me to provide a complete list of citations; the list follows (except, of course, for any sources I couldn't find or forgot along the way).

If you would like to restore this book to the form in which I intended it to be read, simply grab a sharp pair of scissors or a razor blade or box cutter and remove pages 207–221 by cutting along the dotted line.

Who owns the words? Who owns the music and the rest of our culture? We do—all of us—though not all of us know it yet. Reality cannot be copyrighted.

Stop; don't read any farther.

Numbers refer to sections:

2   Sentence about *Unmade Beds*: Soyon Im, "The Good, the Bad, and the Ugly," *Seattle Weekly*

4   Thoreau

5   Roland Barthes, *Barthes by Barthes* (who else would be the author?); "minus the novel": Michael Dirda, "Whispers in the Darkness," *Washington Post*

6   Walter Benjamin, *Arcades Project*

7   Lorraine Adams, "Almost Famous: The Rise of the 'Nobody' Memoir," *Washington Monthly*

8   Mark Willis, "Listening to the Literacy Events of a Blind Reader," http://fairuselab.net/?page_id=635

11   Adams

13   John D'Agata, *The Next American Essay*

16   Second sentence: paraphrase of information conveyed in the foreword to *The New Oxford Annotated Bible*

18   D'Agata

19   D'Agata, in conversation

21–25   Adams

26   William Gass, "The Art of Self," *Harper's*

27   Adams; parenthetical statement: first line, Oliver Wendell Holmes, Jr.; second line: Darwin

28   first half of passage: D'Agata, *The Next American Essay*

29   Gass

32   J. M. Coetzee, *Elizabeth Costello*

33   Adams

34   Jonathan Raban, in conversation

35   Raban assures me that this Greene disclaimer exists, but I can't find it.

36   Vivian Gornick, *The Situation and the Story*

37   Kevin Kelly, "Scan This Book!" *New York Times*

38   D'Agata

39   Alain Robbe-Grillet, *For a New Novel,* the book that in many ways got me thinking about all of this stuff

40   D'Agata

41   Alice Marshall, "The Space Between," unpublished manuscript; cf. last line of my book *Black Planet:* "All that space is the space between us."

42   Kelly

43   Robbe-Grillet

44   Charles Simic, *Dime-Store Alchemy*

45   Adams

48   Ozick, interviewed by Tom Teicholz, *Paris Review*

49   Philip Roth, "Writing American Fiction," *Commentary*

50   Robbe-Grillet

51   D'Agata
52–53 Gornick
55   Jim Paul, "The Found Life," Bread Loaf lecture
57   Geoff Dyer, *Out of Sheer Rage*
58   W. G. Sebald, interviewed by Siegrid Löffler, *Profil*
59   Peter Bailey, "Notes on the Novel-as-Autobiography," in *Novel vs. Fiction,* eds. Jackson I. Cope and Geoffrey Green
63–64 Robert Winder, "Editorial," *Granta*'s "Ambition" issue
65   Ben Marcus, "The Genre Artist," *Believer*
66   Rachel Donadio, "Truth Is Stronger Than Fiction," *New York Times*
67   Margo Jefferson, "It's All in the Family, But Is That Enough?" *New York Times*
69   Saul Steinberg, quoted by Kurt Vonnegut, *A Man Without a Country*
71   Melville, *Billy Budd*
72   D'Agata
73   I'm pretty sure these lines, or something close to these lines, were spoken by Terry Gilliam in an interview, but I can't for the life of me find the source.
74–76 Kelly
77   Robert Greenwald, "Brave New Medium," *Nation*
79   D'Agata
80   Lauren Slater, *Lying*
81   Clifford Irving, interviewed by Mike Wallace on 60 *Minutes*
82   Picasso
84   Slater, quoted in David D. Kirkpatrick, "Questionable Letter for a Liar's Memoir," *New York Times*
85   James Frey
86   Dorothy Gallagher, "Recognizing the Book That Needs to Be Written," *New York Times*
88   First two sentences: Mary Gaitskill, quoted in Joy Press, "The Cult of JT LeRoy," *Village Voice;* the rest is Stephen Beachy, "Who Is the Real JT Leroy?" *New York*
89   Elmyr de Hory, quoted in Orson Welles, *F for Fake*
91   Slater, "One Nation Under the Weather," *Salon*
96   Nic Kelman, quoted in Sara Ivry, "Pick Those Fawning Blurbs Carefully," *New York Times*
101   First three sentences are from Brian Camp's letter to the *New York Times,* "Is It Plagiarism, or Teenage Prose?"; the rest of the passage, except for the last line, is from Malcolm Gladwell, "Annals of Culture," *New Yorker.*
102   Jonathan Lethem, interviewed by Harvey Blume, *Boston Globe*
103   Patricia Hampl, interviewed by Laura Wexler, *AWP Chronicle*
104   Susan Cheever, interviewed by Roberta Brown, *AWP Chronicle*
106   Gornick, "A Memoirist Defends Her Words," *Salon*
108   D'Agata, *The Lost Origins of the Essay*
109   Hampl

110 Gornick, *The Situation and the Story*

113, 115–116 Marshall

119 Except for parenthetical statement, Motoko Rich, "James Frey Collaborating on a Novel for Young Adults, First in a Series," *New York Times*

121 Cicero

122 D'Agata, *The Next American Essay*

124 John Mellencamp (!?)

125 *The Commitments* (the movie version); I haven't read the novel.

126 Hemingway, interviewed by George Plimpton, *Paris Review*

128 First sentence: Lynn Nottage, quoted in Liesl Schillinger, "The Accidental Design of Rolin Jones's Career," *New York Times*

129 Jenni, quoted by Steven Shaviro, *Stranded in the Jungle*—29: http://www.shaviro.com/Stranded/29.html

130 Otto Preminger, (apocryphal?) advice to Lee Remick

131 Thomas Pynchon, *Slow Learner*

132 Ross McElwee, interviewed by Cynthia Lucia, *Cineaste*

133 Dave Eggers, interviewed by Tasha Robinson, *Onion;* Eggers reminds me that he said this ten years ago in a conversation about semi-autobiographical fiction, and that he no longer subscribes to the sentiment expressed here.

134 "funny": title of Rick Reynolds CD; "pretty": title of Steve Martin album

136 Frank O'Hara, quoted in Jim Elledge, *Frank O'Hara*

137 Janette Turner Hospital, *The Last Magician*

138 Robert Lowell, "Epilogue"

139 Robert Towers, review of my novel *Dead Languages* in *New York Review of Books*

141 D'Agata

142 Frederick Barthelme, *The Brothers*

143 Dogme 95 manifesto

144 McElwee

146 Last line: Nietzsche

149 Reynolds, *Only the Truth Is Funny*

151 Martin, quoted in Bruce Weber, "An Arrow Out of the Head and into a Shy Heroine's Heart," *New York Times*

152 Lionel Trilling, *The Liberal Imagination*

153 Adam Gopnik, "Optimist," *New Yorker*

154 First two sentences: Jonathan Goldstein, performing on *This American Life;* I could listen to that self-generating/self-demolishing voice of his forever.

157 Wittgenstein

158 *Walk the Line*

161–162 Patrick Duff, "From the Brink of Oblivion," unpublished manuscript

163 Mark Doty, "Return to Sender," *Writer's Chronicle*

164 Duff

167 David Carr, *The Night of the Gun*

168 Duff

218   Henry Grunwald, *Salinger*

219   A. O. Scott, "A Cock and Bull Story," *New York Times*

220   Stephen Holden, "A Reprieve for Reality in New Crop of Films," *New York Times*

221   Susan Buice, *Four Eyed Monsters*

222   The song "Compared to What," written by Eugene McDaniels, was made famous via recording by Les McCann and Ed Harris at the Montreux Jazz Festival; that record sold more than a million copies. An antiwar and civil rights polemic, the song has recently been retooled by Chicago rapper Common and R & B singer Mya as a Coke commercial.

223   McElwee, *Sherman's March*

225   V. S. Pritchett

226   R. P. Blackmur, *The Expense of Greatness*

228   Jenny Gage, interviewed by Heidi Julavits, *Believer*

230   Robin Hemley, "A Simple Metaphysics," *Conjunctions*

232   No comment

236   McElwee, *Cineaste* interview

242   I was certain this was Frank Rich; I was astonished to find out it was Andrew O'Hehir, "The Long Goodbye," *Salon*

244   Brian Christian, in conversation

246   Patrick Goldstein, "Lovesick Cruise et al. Is Bad Reality TV," *Los Angeles Times*

248   Philip Gourevitch, quoted in Donadio

251   Grégoire Bouillier, *The Mystery Guest*

252   Michael Moore, 2003 Academy Award acceptance speech

253   Anonymous White House aide in first term of Bush 43's administration, quoted in Ron Suskind, "Without a Doubt," *New York Times*

254   Last three sentences: John Hodgman, "Text Message from the Road," *Stranger*

255–257   Stacy Schiff, "The Interactive Truth," *New York Times*

258   Lisa Page, letter to the editor, "In Fiction's Defense," *New York Times*

259   Emerson

260   Commonly attributed to Eliot; put together two statements, one by Eliot and one by Picasso, and you pretty much have it.

261   Picasso

264   Paul D. Miller, aka DJ Spooky, *Rhythm Science*

265   Lloyd Bradley, *Bass Culture*

266   Lee Perry, quoted in Bradley, *This Is Reggae Music*

271   Peter Mountford, "Alistair Wright," unpublished manuscript

273   Jean-Luc Godard, in *Cahiers du Cinéma, 1960–1968,* vol. 2, ed. Jim Hillier

274   Wikipedia entry on Sturtevant

280   Emerson

287 Brian Goedde, "Fake Fan," Experience Music Project Annual Pop Music Conference

288 Lethem

289 Last sentence: Ralph Ellison, *Collected Essays*

290 Goethe

291 Emerson

293 Felicia R. Lee, "An Artist Releases a New Film After Paramount Blocks His First," *New York Times*

295 Last sentence: Liz Robbins, "Artist Admits Using Other Photo for 'Hope' Poster," *New York Times*

297 Charles Baxter, *The Soul Thief*

298 Laurence Sterne, *Tristram Shandy*

299 Borges, "Pierre Menard, Author of the Quixote"

300 Gibson

304 This isn't me; it's James Nugent.

305 Tony DiSanto, quoted in Laura Bly, "The Real Laguna Beach Disdains Its MTV Image," *USA Today*

306 Donadio

307 E. L. Doctorow, quoted in Michiko Kakutani, "Do Facts and Fiction Mix?" *New York Times;* the parenthetical comment is mine (shocker).

308 Marshall

310 Steve Almond, *Not That You Asked;* last line: Peter Brooks, *Realist Vision*

312 James Joyce

313 Sebald

314 Donald Kuspit, "Collage: The Organizing Principle of Art in the Age of the Relativity of Art," in *Relativism in the Arts,* ed. Betty Jean Craige

315 Daniel Dennett, *Consciousness Explained*

316 Kuspit

317 Ronald Sukenick, *Out*

319 Lance Olsen, *10:01*

320 M. H. Abrams and Jack Stillinger, eds., John Stuart Mill: *Autobiography and Literary Essays*

323 Djuna Barnes, *Nightwood*

326 Lorrie Moore, *Self-Help*

329 Thomas Sobchack and Vivian Carol Sobchack, *An Introduction to Film*

332 Picasso

333 Sounds to me like Julian Schnabel, but that might just be because of the broken dishes.

335 Attributed to Charlie Parker by Andrew Hill in Ben Ratliff, *The Jazz Ear*

336 Walter Pater, *The Renaissance*

337 Nicholson Baker, *U and I*

338 Sven Birkerts, *American Energies*

339 Nina Michelson, "Silence and Music," unpublished manuscript

340–341 Simic

342–343 Michelson

344 Simic

345 Thomas Lux, "Triptych, Middle Panel Burning"

346 Deborah Eisenberg, "Resistance," in Frank Conroy, ed., *The Eleventh Draft*

348–349 Michelson

352 Benjamin

353 Emerson

354 Olsen, "Notes Toward the Musicality of Creative Disjunction," *Symploke*

355 Emerson

356 First sentence: Emerson; the rest: Goethe

357 Walter Murch, quoted in Michael Ondaatje and Walter Murch, *The Conversations*

358 Theodor Adorno

359 David Markson, *Reader's Block*

362 Annie Dillard, *Holy the Firm*

363 Viktor Shklovsky, *Theory of Prose*

364 International Museum of Collage, Assemblage, and Construction (http://collagemuseum.com/COLLAGE-signs-surfaces/index.html)

365 Gopnik, "What Comes Naturally," *New Yorker*

366 D'Agata, interviewed by Carey Smith, *Collision*

368 First sentence: Eliot, *The Waste Land*

369 Robert Dana, interviewed by Lowell Jaeger, *Poets & Writers Magazine*

370 Marcus

372 Ellen Bryant Voigt, "Narrative and Lyric," *Southern Review*

373 Elvis Mitchell, "Fast Food, Fast Women," *New York Times*

374 Svenja Soldovieri, in conversation

376 Shklovsky

377 David Mamet, "Hearing the Notes That Aren't Played," *New York Times*

378 Ezra Pound, *ABC of Reading*

380 Conversation between Janet Malcolm and David Salle, from her profile of him, "Forty-one False Starts," *New Yorker*

382 Emerson

383 Nietzsche

384 D'Agata and Deborah Tall, "The Lyric Essay," *Seneca Review*

385 Paul

386 D'Agata, in conversation

388 Lines 1 and 2: Rebecca Solnit, *Eve Said to the Serpent;* lines three to five, Dyer, *Out of Sheer Rage;* line 6: Solnit, *A Field Guide to Getting Lost*

389 Malcolm, "The Silent Woman," *New Yorker*

390 Ozick, introduction to *Best American Essays 1998*

391 Phillip Lopate, *The Art of the Personal Essay*

392 Orwell

458 Nabokov, *Lolita;* in honor of the author's Olympian hauteur, I corrected the grammar and punctuation.

459 Borges

461 Coetzee, *Doubling the Point*

462 Oscar Wilde

467 Smith

468 New York Film Festival catalogue copy

469 Emerson

470 Yeats

472 Wilde, preface to *The Picture of Dorian Gray*

474 Gornick

475 James Shapiro, "The Critic's Teeth," *New York Times;* Shapiro and I were colleagues on the National Book Award nonfiction panel a few years ago: all five of us utterly disagreed about what nonfiction was.

476 Samuel Butler

477 Anne Carson, *Glass, Irony, and God*

478 Emerson

479 Raban, Powells.com interview

480 Montaigne

481 McElwee, *Cineaste* interview

482 Verlyn Klinkenborg, "Carson, Night by Night," *New York Times*

483 Lorin Stein, "Loves of the Lambs," *New York Review of Books*

484 Dan Georgakas, "The Art of Autobiography," *Cineaste*

485 Dickinson

488 Lopate

489 Yeats

491 Marshall

492 My crush? Sort of; more Paul Bravmann's.

493 Mikhail Lermontov, *A Hero of Our Time*

494 George Bernard Shaw

495 Dana

496 Dyer, self-interview

498 Keats

499 Emerson

501 Montaigne

502 Ad copy for *Curb Your Enthusiasm*

510 My girlfriend and I shared the house with her brother; it was actually he who was wildly prolific all summer. Makes a better story the other way, though.

524–525 Alexis de Tocqueville, *Democracy in America*

526 László Kardos, quoted in *More Reflections on the Meaning of Life,* ed. David Friend

527 Can't quite remember where this is from, though it sounds like fourth-generation Sartre. Endless is the quest for truth.

528 Nietzsche

529 Woody Allen, *Side Effects*
530 Tennessee Williams, preface to *Cat on a Hot Tin Roof*
531 Zadie Smith, "The Limited Circle Is Pure," *New Republic;*
     "information bureau . . .": Adorno
532 Nietzsche
533 Nirvana, "All Apologies"
534 Schopenhauer
535 Nabokov, *Pnin*
538 Virginia Woolf, *A Room of One's Own*
539 Jean Cocteau
540 Robert Rauschenberg, quoted in Michael Kimmelman,
     "Robert Rauschenberg, American Artist, Dies at 82," *New
     York Times*
541 Steinberg, quoted in Vonnegut
542 Denis Johnson, in conversation
543 Saul Bellow, "What Kind of Day Did You Have?"
544 Fitzgerald, *The Great Gatsby*
545 Barry Hannah, interviewed by James D. Lilley and Brion
     Oberkirch, *Mississippi Review*
546 Jennifer Jason Leigh, quoted in Sylviane Gold, "Ready to Play
     Anyone but Herself," *New York Times*
547 Paul Elie, *The Life You Save May Be Your Own*
548 Hass
549 Emerson
550 Adam Phillips, *Equals*
551 Bellow, quoted at
     http://web.israelinsider.com/Articles/Culture/5286.htm
552 Beckett
554 Jim McBride, *David Holzman's Diary*
555 Robert Capa
556 Kierkegaard
557 Gass
558 Dillard, in praise of Maggie Nelson's *The Red Parts*
559 Gordon Lish, quoted in Amy Hempel, "Captain Fiction,"
     Vanity Fair
560 D. H. Lawrence
561 Yeats
562 Emerson
563 Thomas Mann, *Tonio Kruger*
564 Lopate
565 Ruth Behar, *The Vulnerable Observer*
566 Flaubert, *The Writing Life*
567 Antonin Artaud, *The Theater and Its Double*
569 Bob Dylan, "Outlaw Blues"
570 *The Wild Ones*
571 *King Lear*
572 da Vinci

573   Prokofiev

574   Michelangelo

575   Nicholas Perricone, quoted in Alex Witchel, "Perriconology," *New York Times Magazine*

576   Vikram Chandra, quoted in Motoko Rich, "Digital Publishing Is Scrambling the Industry's Rules," *New York Times*

577   Goethe

588   O'Brien

589   Naipaul, quoted in James Wood, "Wounder and Wounded," *New Yorker*

590   First sentence: Benjamin

591   Richard Serra, quoted in Kimmelman, "At the Met and the Modern with Richard Serra," *New York Times*

592   Dyer

596   Marcus, "Why Experimental Fiction Threatens to Destroy Publishing, Jonathan Franzen, and Life as We Know It," *Harper's*

597   Robbe-Grillet

598   Gornick

599   Hannah

601   Williams, *Spring and All*

602   Coetzee, *Summertime*

603   Williams

604   Gornick

605   Sebald

606   All but last sentence: Naipaul, quoted in Donadio, "The Irascible Prophet," *New York Times*

607–608   Lopate

609   First five sentences except titles: D'Agata, *Collision* interview

610   Dyer, *Out of Sheer Rage*

611   Except for titles, E. M. Cioran, *The Temptation to Exist*

612   D'Agata, *The Next American Essay*

613   Plutarch

614   Emerson

615   Gornick

616   Marcus, "The Genre Artist," *Believer*

617   Berger, *G*

618   Carson, *Decreation*

ALSO BY DAVID SHIELDS

"Shields is a sharp-eyed, self-deprecating, and at times hilarious writer."
—The Wall Street Journal

THE THING ABOUT LIFE IS THAT
ONE DAY YOU'LL BE DEAD

Mesmerized and somewhat unnerved by his 97-year-old father's vitality and optimism, David Shields undertakes an original investigation of our flesh-and-blood existence, our mortal being. Weaving together personal anecdote, biological fact, philosophical doubt, cultural criticism, and the wisdom of an eclectic range of writers and thinkers—from Lucretius to Woody Allen—Shields expertly renders both a hilarious family portrait and a truly resonant meditation on mortality. *The Thing About Life* provokes us to contemplate the brevity and radiance of our own sojourn on earth and challenges us to rearrange our thinking in crucial and unexpected ways.

Memoir/978-0-307-38796-7